The Lifegiving Parent Experience

THE *Life* GIVING PARENT experience

A 10-WEEK JOURNEY OF PARENTING FOR LIFE

CLAY & SALLY CLARKSON

TYNDALE
MOMENTUM®

The nonfiction imprint of
Tyndale House Publishers, Inc.

Visit Tyndale online at www.tyndale.com.

Visit Tyndale Momentum online at www.tyndalemomentum.com.

Visit Clay Clarkson at www.wholeheart.org.

Visit Sally Clarkson at www.sallyclarkson.com, www.momheart.com, and www.wholeheart.org.

TYNDALE, *Tyndale Momentum*, and Tyndale's quill logo are registered trademarks of Tyndale House Publishers, Inc. The Tyndale Momentum logo is a trademark of Tyndale House Publishers, Inc. Tyndale Momentum is the nonfiction imprint of Tyndale House Publishers, Inc., Carol Stream, Illinois.

The Lifegiving Parent Experience: A 10-Week Journey of Parenting for Life

Designed by Julie Chen

Unless otherwise indicated, all Scripture quotations are taken from the *Holy Bible*, New Living Translation, copyright © 1996, 2004, 2015 by Tyndale House Foundation. Used by permission of Tyndale House Publishers, Inc., Carol Stream, Illinois 60188. All rights reserved.

Scripture quotations marked NASB are taken from the New American Standard Bible,® copyright © 1960, 1962, 1963, 1968, 1971, 1972, 1973, 1975, 1977, 1995 by The Lockman Foundation. Used by permission.

Scripture quotations marked NET© are used by permission and taken from the NET Bible,® copyright © 1996–2006 by Biblical Studies Press, L.L.C., http://netbible.com. All rights reserved.

Scripture quotations marked NIV are taken from the Holy Bible, *New International Version*,® *NIV*.® Copyright © 1973, 1978, 1984, 2011 by Biblica, Inc.® Used by permission. All rights reserved worldwide.

For information about special discounts for bulk purchases, please contact Tyndale House Publishers at csresponse@tyndale.com, or call 1-800-323-9400.

ISBN 978-1-4964-2279-8

Printed in the United States of America

24	23	22	21	20	19	18
7	6	5	4	3	2	1

Contents

Introduction *vii*

Introduction

Christian parenting is not meant to be a solo or silo experience—Mom and Dad taking care of parenting business in their own home in their own way, and taking care not to make their parenting anyone else's business. If we're honest, as parents we can all become insecure at some point about what we're doing, how we're doing it, and if we're doing enough. We're understandably reticent to open our homes' "silo doors" to give others an inside view, especially of how our faith gets worked out in our family life and worked into our children's lives.

Sally and I totally understand. As parents of four now-grown children, we've experienced more than thirty years of being there and doing that in our own home silo. We've lived through all the same feelings, fears, foibles, and faith challenges that every Christian parent experiences. It's been a wild and wonderful journey for us, just as we're sure it has been and will be for you. And we can say from this end of the journey that it's been worth it every step of the way, or at least most of them. But it's a journey you'll definitely want to make with friends—there's just no substitute for having a parenting posse to share the trip. This group study guide will start you on that adventure.

Before going further, though, let's be clear about what this study guide is *not*. First, it's not a guided guilt trip to make you feel bad about what you're not doing as a Christian parent. Most of us don't need any help with that. Second, it's not a laundry list of things you need to do to be a "successful" Christian parent. That list does not exist, either in the Bible or in a book. Finally, it's not just an "important stuff God says about parenting" doctrinal survey. There are lots of books for that.

So, then, what is *The Lifegiving Parent Experience*? Let's just say it's an itinerary. It's a ten-week journey with friends along the path of parenting, with stops along the way to ponder and discuss what we've been learning. Everybody experiences road trips differently, just as we all experience the journey of parenting differently. This study guide is a friendly way for you to take some mental snapshots, make some helpful notes about the places we'll stop on this trip together, and take it all back home to show your kids. This journey is all about becoming what we call a lifegiving parent.

What Is Lifegiving Parenting?

Lifegiving parenting, simply defined, is about bringing the life of God into your home—giving the life of God and the God of life to your children. As we say in our book *The Lifegiving Parent*, it's about opening the doors, windows, and vents of your home to let in the love, light, and life of God. He wants to be there, to come in and be a part of the life of your home. Lifegiving parenting is not about doing parenting a certain way but about making ways for the living God to enter into your home. Lifegiving parenting is not a set of rules or a surefire formula, but simply a way of life.

Why is that important? We've found through the years that many well-meaning Christian parents fall into the trap of thinking they have a Christian home because of what their children are doing—going to Sunday school and Bible club, listening to Christian music, watching Christian videos, going to Christian activities. There's nothing wrong with any of those things, but the reality is that a Christian home can never be defined by what the children are doing but only by what the parents are doing. Your children cannot make your home Christian; only you can do that. Many parents do well at giving their children what we call the Christian life but fail to give them the life of Christ. Lifegiving parenting is a way of helping you make sure your children experience the life of the living God in your home.

What Is the Purpose of This Study Guide?

This companion Bible study and discussion guide for *The Lifegiving Parent* can be used either individually for personal reflection or in a small group for interaction and mutual encouragement. However, we suggest that you gather several other couples who are parents and go through the study together. Whether you find friends your own age or bring together couples of a variety of ages, the benefits will be the same—sharing the parenting journey, talking about God's Word together, and helping one another become lifegiving parents.

We don't think of *The Lifegiving Parent Experience* as just a book of formal Bible lessons. Instead, we see it as a guide for an informal discussion group for Christian parents. We want it to be the road map for a meaningful and enjoyable spiritual journey with friends, not a curriculum for serious and sober study. We've tried to make the weekly discussion content interesting, insightful, and interactive, yet also something you can do in a comfortable amount of time with little or no preparation. You should be able to complete each weekly study in about ninety minutes, depending on how long you spend in discussion and prayer. The study and discussion questions are written to give everyone in the group freedom and encouragement to contribute their thoughts, insights, and experiences.

The L.I.F.E. outline used for each of the ten weekly studies is designed to move your group discussion from general ideas to specifics. It's an approach that allows you to start with a friendly "warm-up" to the subject before moving into reading and discussing relevant Scriptures and then personalizing and praying about what you've been discussing. We've chosen to use the New Living Translation (NLT) for most of the "Interact with the Word" Bible passages because of its easy readability and more conversational vocabulary for group discussion.

Here's the weekly outline, with suggested times, based on the acrostic L.I.F.E.:

L **Listen to a Story** (twenty minutes)—Each week begins with "A Lifegiving Parenting Moment," which is read aloud to the group and then discussed. This brief story will illustrate an aspect of the lifegiving topic for the week through a creatively written vignette about Christian parenting, with suggested questions to guide discussion. This is the "warm-up" discussion to get everybody on the same page.

I **Interact with the Word** (thirty minutes)—Three relevant Bible passages are provided to be read aloud and discussed by the group. "Word Notes" for each Scripture provide some biblical context and commentary, and suggested questions will help focus the group discussion. You're free to discuss all or just some of the passages depending on time available.

F **Focus on Parenting** (twenty minutes)—This section begins with an excerpt and brief summary of the subject of the corresponding chapter in *The*

Lifegiving Parent, with guidance for writing down some ways, in the space provided, that parents might consider living out the lifegiving principle for that week in their own homes. Everyone's ideas are then shared with the group and discussed.

E　**Engage with God** (twenty minutes)—Finally, prayer requests related to the lifegiving principle, or heartbeat, for that week are shared with the group. Prayer suggestions are provided to help you get started. This is real-time application of what has been studied and discussed—engaging in prayer with God about what has been learned and asking Him to help you make it a reality in your life.

The group is not just about study and discussion, though. It's also about relationships. Before and after the formal group meeting time, allow informal time for sharing life through friendship, fellowship, and food. Getting through the content of this study guide is not the only goal of your time together with other parents. You're also building relationships by sharing the common bond you enjoy in Christ to "think of ways to motivate one another to acts of love and good works" (Hebrews 10:24). And as Jesus said, "Where two or three gather together as my followers, I am there among them" (Matthew 18:20). He was expressing the principle of spiritual unity that Paul would later express as the *koinonia*, or fellowship, of the body of Christ. When you develop relationships as Spirit-led believers, you are bringing the life of Christ into your group. That means engaging in biblical fellowship as a group is practice for being a lifegiving parent at home.

So call some friends, make some dates, and begin your journey together as lifegiving parents. If you're not certain how to start and lead a small group, review the "Meeting as a Lifegiving Parents Group" suggestions at the back of the book to help you get started. Let this study guide be your itinerary for a mutual journey into lifegiving parenting, and let it lead you into a new way of thinking about your home and children. May your time together of fellowship, study, and discussion put you on the path to a lifegiving parenting experience that will change you, your children, and even generations of your family yet to come.

Clay and Sally Clarkson

Perhaps you're continuing a journey you're already on and are just looking for new parenting ideas. Perhaps you're stepping onto the path of lifegiving parenting for the first time, looking for God's direction for your home. Or perhaps you're considering a new paradigm for your Christian home—moving from a legalistic model of form and function to a lifegiving model of faith and freedom. However you come to lifegiving parenting, and whatever it leads you to do in your home, keep Paul's admonition in mind: "The Lord is the Spirit, and where the Spirit of the Lord is, there is freedom" (2 Corinthians 3:17, NIV). You're free in God's Spirit to discover what is right for your home.

From *The Lifegiving Parent*

SOMEONE'S GOT TO GIVE

*Thus says the LORD, "Stand by the ways and see and
ask for the ancient paths, where the good way is, and
walk in it; and you will find rest for your souls."*
JEREMIAH 6:16, NASB

From The Lifegiving Parent, *chapter 1*

*Only you—parents alive in Christ because of the Holy Spirit
within you—have the ability and the power of the Spirit to
make your home a Christian home. Engagement with Christian
culture does not define a Christian home; engagement with the
living Christ does. That understanding is a necessary first step
on the path to becoming a lifegiving parent.*

Thoughts on "Someone's Got to Give"

Though contemporary culture is changing life all around us, it
doesn't have to change us, and it can't change what has always
been true about God—including the foundational biblical

3

truths about His design for family. We believe God lives within us, by His Spirit and within our homes, through our faith and trust. Even as winds of culture howl around our children, our fundamental responsibility is to give them the life of God that we have found in Him. That is what we call lifegiving parenting. This week's study is about our responsibility to give our children the life of the living God in our homes and families.

Talking through L.I.F.E. Together

L *Listen to a Story*
A LIFEGIVING PARENTING MOMENT:

ABOUT CHOICES AND CHANGES

Josh and Molly McPherson married in their respectably late twenties and started their family soon after. They've both already turned a hard corner on forty, and they're feeling the burn of a too-often too-busy life. They're firmly planted in "the house that Josh built," which they christened early on simply as McPherson Manor. They built a large house not knowing how many children God would give them, so with four under their roof now, they're all settled and comfortable with the life they've created.

Josh McPherson is one of the good guys—a decent man who loves his wife and kids and works hard to make a good life for them. Josh struggles to balance work and family, but he never gives up, and he meets with other men to stay accountable to his priorities as a husband and father. Even though he's never been to Scotland, he loves his Scottish heritage and often claims, with a bad brogue, "Aye, I hae some Scottish bluid in me," suggesting it makes him a better man. Whether that's true or not, he's capable, confident, honest, and loyal—just the kind of contractor you'd want to work with to build your home. His gray-tinged dark hair and easy smile perfectly match his genial nature. Josh custom builds one house at a time so he can be available to its future family. As he says, "I'm not just a house builder; I'm a home creator."

Molly is the warm relational core of the McPherson clan. Her classy-casual naturalness in look and dress softens her fiercely loving and protective demeanor. She can be found alone with tea or engaging a child in one of the many cozy nooks, bay window seats, and comfy corners she insisted Josh include in their house plans. Molly has blogged for the past five years at *Molly in the Middle* about the joys and challenges of being a midlife wife and mother. She writes personal and helpful stories about her home and community life, as well as inspirational insights from Scripture, but it's the vulnerable posts about her failings and weaknesses that always get the most likes and shares. She's also an amateur still life photographer and longs to write a book about the home, but she's still chasing the elusive publishing contract. Until that happens, she's content just sharing her life and photography on the blog and working on a book for herself and her friends.

Molly and Josh both are feeling the reality check of the soon-to-arrive end of childhood for Gracie, their firstborn. Molly is more than ready to be the fun mom of a teen girl, but it will be uncharted waters. The sweetly innocent Gracie is everything they could have wanted for a first McPherson child. But now at twelve years old, she will soon leave childhood behind to become the first family teenager, and the signs of that impending change are beginning to find expression in her thoughts and emotions. Still waters run deep in the introverted Gracie, and she is leaning into young adulthood with both anticipation and quiet trepidation.

The nine-year-old twins, David and Amy, are almost as easy as having just one middle child. They get along reasonably well, enjoy each other most of the time, and generally don't rock the boat. They're at that fascinating age when they can express real, albeit immature and sometimes challenging, opinions and feelings. Six-year-old Tyler James, or T. J., as he prefers to be called, is in full boyhood mode—active and verbal with a never-satisfied curiosity. He's their official hands-on handful, a delightful and fun-loving but sometimes boat-rocking child.

It's been a busy summer and fall for everyone—a large custom home for Josh; ongoing work on a book of stories, recipes, and photographs for Molly; summer and school activities and friends for the kids. It just seems there's been no stopping place for anyone. No time to be a family and spend time with each other, make memories, or hear from God. Josh and Molly both knew it was time to make some changes, so they asked his parents to watch the kids while they got away for the weekend at a lodge in the mountains nearby. They needed undistracted time just to talk about where they were in life—about their marriage, their hopes and dreams, what their children needed from them, and their relationships with God.

Being away together gave them relaxed, unhurried time to unpack all the things they had not discussed in recent months. As they talked about raising their children, they both felt convicted by the Spirit that they could do better. They knew that the window of childhood was brief, and they needed to be intentional as Christian parents. Over the weekend they prayed for each of their children, but more than anything else they prayed for themselves. They asked God to help them become the kind of lifegiving parents they wanted to be. They asked for more of His life in them to give to their children.

- *Just for Fun:* How is the McPherson family like your family? How is your family different? How would you describe your children? What are some of their strengths and weaknesses?

- What would you talk about on a weekend getaway with your spouse? What hopes and dreams would you share? What plans would you make as parents for your family and children?

I Interact with the Word
TRUTHS ABOUT "SOMEONE'S GOT TO GIVE"

MATTHEW 7:24-27 | *Building on a firm foundation*

Anyone who listens to my teaching and follows
it is wise, like a person who builds a house on
solid rock. Though the rain comes in torrents and

the floodwaters rise and the winds beat against
that house, it won't collapse because it is built on
bedrock. But anyone who hears my teaching and
doesn't obey it is foolish, like a person who builds a
house on sand. When the rains and floods come and
the winds beat against that house, it will collapse
with a mighty crash.

Word Notes: On a hill in the rolling countryside of northern
Israel, surrounded by His disciples and a large crowd of followers, Jesus preaches His Sermon on the Mount. He talks
about the law, what it means to be His disciple, and how the
inbreaking Kingdom of God will change everything. At the
end of His sermon, He describes two kinds of people based
on how they respond to His teaching.

1. Each of the persons Jesus describes "listens to" (literally,
    "hears") what He is teaching, but only the one who
    "follows" (literally, "does") His teaching is called "wise."
    How can we make sure as parents that we are not the
    foolish listeners of Jesus who hear but don't obey? How
    do we make sure we're the wise doers?

2. In what ways have you found, especially in your par-
    enting, that Jesus' teaching is like a "solid rock"? What

kinds of rains, floods, and winds have come against your house that might have negatively affected your parenting, but didn't because you listened to Jesus and were wise?

3. If you're brave enough to share (you're among friends!), describe a way you once tried to build part of your parenting house on sand and suffered consequences. Remember that doing a foolish thing does not make you a foolish person. How can we protect ourselves from foolish parenting choices in the future?

JEREMIAH 6:16 | *Choosing the proven path*

This is what the LORD says: "Stop at the crossroads and look around. Ask for the old, godly way, and walk in it. Travel its path, and you will find rest for your souls. But you reply, 'No, that's not the road we want!'"

Word Notes: Jeremiah is God's prophet to the remaining two tribes in Judah. Four hundred years earlier, when Israel's twelve tribes were united and strong, David asked, "If the foundations are destroyed, what can the righteous do?" (Psalm 11:3,

NASB). Though Jeremiah is prophesying that God's judgment and destruction are soon to come from Babylon, he still provides a positive answer to David's question.

1. What are the crossroads you find yourself at as a parent in today's culture? When you take the time to stop and look around, what sorts of choices and temptations are you faced with that could keep you from giving your child God's life?

2. What is the "old, godly way" (or "ancient paths," NASB) that Jeremiah says we should walk in? How might that be an answer to David's question about foundations? Who are we supposed to "ask" about that way, and what would it mean to "walk in it" as a parent today?

3. What does it mean to find rest for your soul? As a parent, in what specific and practical ways would you find rest by traveling that path? Why would a parent choose

not to travel that path in today's world? Would any of those reasons tempt you not to?

DEUTERONOMY 6:4-9 | *Old words good for all of God's families*

Listen, O Israel! The LORD is our God, the LORD alone. And you must love the LORD your God with all your heart, all your soul, and all your strength. And you must commit yourselves wholeheartedly to these commands that I am giving you today. Repeat them again and again to your children. Talk about them when you are at home and when you are on the road, when you are going to bed and when you are getting up. Tie them to your hands and wear them on your forehead as reminders. Write them on the doorposts of your house and on your gates.

Word Notes: Israel is a nation with a law, looking at last into the land promised to Abraham by God five hundred years earlier. Before they cross the Jordan River and go into the land, Moses reads the law and gives the people of Israel the words that will define their identity and purpose for millennia to come. It's called the Shema ("hear"), a call to be a unified nation of faithful families following the one true God.

1. Moses is addressing his command to the families of Israel. As a parent, how do you help your family love God completely, with all their hearts, souls, and strength? Are there ways that you see your family not loving God? How is loving God about feeling or doing?

2. Moses told the parents of Israel they must be committed to God's commands so they could give those commands to their children. Describe how parents might try to teach their children's hearts truths of God that they do not first fully understand. How are you diligent to continually teach God's truth to your children?

3. Moses' words about places and times combine to create a Hebrew parallelism that means the Israelites were to teach God's truth everywhere and all the time— in other words, there was no place or time where it shouldn't be happening. How can you, as a parent, do

that today? How can your life and home reflect God's truth for your children?

F Focus on Parenting
PLANS FOR "SOMEONE'S GOT TO GIVE"

FROM THE LIFEGIVING PARENT, *CHAPTER 1*

If lifegiving parenting is about giving our children real life in God so they can be fully alive in Him, then . . . someone's got to give. That transfer of the life of God to our children does not happen just by good intent or by accident. It happens for one reason only—because we decide that we are the people who've got to give. Not another person, group, or church; not an organization, resource, or influence . . . just us. We are the lifegivers. We are the ones who will give the life of God to our children.

MAKE LIFEGIVING PLANS FOR YOUR FAMILY

As Moses suggests in the Shema, you need to prepare your own heart to be a lifegiving parent so that you will have life to give to your children. Write down ways that you can become the lifegiving parent God wants you to be—things to add to your life or take away, habits to begin or break, skills to learn, decisions to make. Remember, you must *have* God's life to *give* God's life to your children. As a group, share and compare your ideas for becoming a lifegiving parent.

E | *Engage with God*
PRAYERS FOR "SOMEONE'S GOT TO GIVE"

Share prayer requests related to the concepts you've discussed this week. Then move into a time of group prayer, letting these prompts direct you:

- ※ Lord, give us hearts to do whatever is necessary to give our children Your life.

- ※ Strengthen us to choose to build our houses upon the rock of Your words and wisdom.

- ※ Direct our steps onto the "old, godly way" where we will find a strong foundation.

- ※ Help us to impress Your truth on our hearts so we can impress it on our children's hearts.

- ※ Discipline us to teach our children diligently— everywhere, all the time, and in every way.

NUMBERING YOUR CHILD'S DAYS

*Teach us to number our days, that we may
present to You a heart of wisdom.*

PSALM 90:12, NASB

From The Lifegiving Parent, *chapter 2*

*The reality is that you have only about a ten-year window with
each of your children to prepare them for the remaining decades
of their lives. In childhood, you can form their values, attitudes,
and character; as they enter young adulthood (their teens), your
influence and instruction will begin to set in their hearts and
minds; as they enter adulthood, your influence lessens as who
they are becomes more settled.*

Thoughts on Numbering Your Child's Days

The first of what we call the eight "Heartbeats of Parental
Lifegiving" is numbering your child's days, not because of the

idea that planning should precede doing, but because vision should define direction. We "start with the end in mind" because what we envision will determine what we endeavor. The ten-year window of childhood from four to fourteen is brief, which is why you need to number your children's days—help them use time well and set goals with pleasing God in mind. But even more, you need to number your own days as a parent and as a disciple of Jesus Christ in order to reach the end that God has in mind—and that He wants you to have in mind—for your children.

Talking through L.I.F.E. Together

L | Listen to a Story
A LIFEGIVING PARENTING MOMENT:

ABOUT DAYS AND DETAILS

The weekend in the mountains with Molly went by too quickly. Josh loved having that casual time alone with his wife to relax, eat dinner out without the kids, and talk and pray about their life together without interruptions. He smiled, recalling that he'd actually written down a few simple plans and ideas for their marriage and family. He thought he should share them with Molly. But then he remembered . . . it was Monday again, he was in his office, and the gears of "real" life engaged with a jarring jolt. Molly would have to come later. Back to work.

As he shuffled some papers and architectural drawings on his large planning table, he distractedly wondered what Molly and the kids would be doing today. "Focus, Josh. Focus. This house is not going to build itself," he chided himself out loud. The large custom home he'd been working on for the past ten months was getting close to completion, but he knew he couldn't let himself fall behind schedule on what still needed to be done. He started thinking about dates and deadlines. Josh was as proficient on his laptop and connected gadgets as the next guy, but he always defaulted to pencil and paper when it came to getting planning details out of his mind quickly.

Every house he built was like a human body to Josh— bone, blood, flesh, and spirit. Bone was everything structural, blood was all the utilities, flesh was the cosmetics, and spirit was the extra touches that helped make the house into a home. At this point, only flesh and spirit were left to do on the RBH (short for the "Really Big House") project. He pulled out the graph paper Moleskine notebook he carried around and began to write down several dozen tasks that were still in process or yet to be started. As he wrote, he added a current completion percentage and a time goal for each task. He'd jotted down well over a dozen tasks when something inside made him stop writing. Something bothered him, and he wasn't sure what it was.

His mind went back to the weekend with Molly, and he remembered again the list of plans he had made while they talked. *I know that list has at least a dozen good ideas*, he thought to himself as he flipped to the very back of his notebook where he'd written them down at the lodge. When he got there, he found just nine lines of simple, undated things he wanted to do with his family. There wasn't much detail—nothing like his work planning. Then, in some kind of epiphany-like moment, it occurred to him: If he was so good at making plans to build physical homes, why wasn't he doing the same thing for building his spiritual home? He did this every day at work, almost as second nature, but it took him months and a weekend away to think about building his own home—the very real bone, blood, flesh, and spirit he was building in the lives of his children.

Josh was not the emotional type, but conviction from God can be as emotional as it is mental, and the significance of this realization caught in his throat. "Busted," he said out loud again (he often talked to himself in his private office). "Lord, I get it. And I'm sorry. You need to help me get this right." He closed the notebook, picked up his cell phone, and hit the speed dial for Molly. She always took Josh's call when she saw his name come up on her screen.

"Hey, Moll. What're you doing right now? . . . Well, can you spare some time this afternoon? We need to continue a conversation we started up at the lodge. . . . No, no, not about us. Well, yeah, I guess it is about us. But we're good. I just want to talk more about our children. About . . . well, about family planning. No, not that kind of family planning. I mean planning about building our home, our children."

Molly, always up for a serious talk over coffee, said the

older kids were at activities until five, and she could arrange for T. J. to play at his friend's house next door. "You have my attention. Let's talk."

Josh ended the call and thought out loud, "And God, You have my attention. I hope You'll join us for coffee."

- *Just for Fun:* Do you ever talk to yourself out loud, and if you do, what do you say? Do you talk to God out loud? How would you say building a physical house is like building your spiritual home?

- Have you ever had an "epiphany-like moment" about parenting? What was it about? Did you feel like the Spirit was convicting you? What did you do about it?

I Interact with the Word
TRUTHS ABOUT NUMBERING YOUR CHILD'S DAYS

PSALM 90:2, 4, 10, 12, 17 | *Choosing to number your days*

Before the mountains were born or You gave birth to the earth and the world, even from everlasting to everlasting, You are God. . . . For a thousand years in Your sight are like yesterday when it passes by, or as a watch in the night. . . . As for the days of our life, they contain seventy years, or if due to strength, eighty years, yet their pride is but labor and sorrow; for soon it is gone and we fly away. . . . So teach us to number our days, that we may present to You a

heart of wisdom. . . . Let the favor of the Lord our
God be upon us; and confirm for us the work of our
hands; yes, confirm the work of our hands. (NASB)

Word Notes: Psalm 90 is attributed to Moses, who was used
by God to free Israel from captivity in Egypt about five
hundred years before David lived. He acknowledges God's
eternal nature, decries humanity's brevity, and asks for God's
favor on His servants. In light of the transitoriness of life,
Moses prays that God will show His people how to live their
days wisely and well for Him and that He will make their
work meaningful.

1. How do you make sense of God's eternal nature
    ("from everlasting to everlasting, You are God," v. 2)?
    In one of his letters, Peter refers to Moses' words in
    verse 4 to say God is not slow about keeping His
    promises (see 2 Peter 3:8-9). How does "a thousand
    years is like a day" cause you to think about our time
    on earth?

2. Does seventy or eighty years seem like enough time to
    please God during your life on earth? If our days are
    soon "gone and we fly away," how should you think
    about life? If you pray, like Moses, "Teach us to num-

ber our days" (v. 12), what does that mean? Are you doing that at this point in your life?

3. Numbering our days enables us to "present to [God] a heart of wisdom" (v. 12). What is the relationship between planning and wisdom? Is having a "heart of wisdom" the same as doing wise things? What efforts (or works) as a parent do you want God to approve and make successful in your life?

LUKE 14:27-30 | *Planning to be a disciple*

If you do not carry your own cross and follow me, you cannot be my disciple. But don't begin until you count the cost. For who would begin construction of a building without first calculating the cost to see if there is enough money to finish it? Otherwise, you might complete only the foundation before running out of money, and then everyone would laugh at you. They would say, "There's the person who started that building and couldn't afford to finish it!"

Word Notes: Luke alone records this account of Jesus' teaching about discipleship. He says that Jesus was moving from one village to another, teaching and preaching on His way to Jerusalem, when He turned around, probably suddenly, and challenged the commitment of those following Him. He spoke provocatively in order to make them realize that being His disciple would require a sacrifice.

1. Jesus didn't waste words. Those following Him knew what a Roman cross represented—a slow, painful death. Being willing to endure that kind of hardship would be part of being His disciple. What equivalent expression today would make you stop and listen to Jesus? What does it mean to "carry your own cross and follow [Him]"?

2. Were you ever challenged to "count the cost" before you became a follower, or disciple, of Jesus? Did you ever calculate what the personal cost might be for following Him? What have the costs been for you? Do you feel now that you have the spiritual capital to complete what you started?

3. As a disciple of Jesus, how does His illustration apply to you as a parent? How is the construction of a home and family similar to the construction of a building? Before you started having children, how did you count the cost to be sure you would have the resources to be a faithful parent?

EPHESIANS 5:15-18 | *Setting free your time for God*

Be careful how you live. Don't live like fools, but like those who are wise. Make the most of every opportunity in these evil days. Don't act thoughtlessly, but understand what the Lord wants you to do. Don't be drunk with wine, because that will ruin your life. Instead, be filled with the Holy Spirit.

Word Notes: Paul wrote the Ephesian letter to be read to churches throughout Asia Minor. It is a visionary letter written to give believers a high view of God's eternal purpose and grace for the church. In this section of the letter, which begins with chapter 4, he's explaining what it means to "walk" with Christ. This brief passage is part of a litany of admonitions about the Christian life.

1. Paul admonishes readers, literally, to "watch how they're walking," alluding to the warning in Proverbs that we should live not unwisely (as fools) but wisely. Are the choices we make in life as stark as Paul suggests? Even as well-intentioned Christian parents, how can we walk unwisely? How can we be sure to walk wisely?

2. We should "make the most of every opportunity." Literally, Paul tells readers to be continually redeeming this season of life (purchasing it out of slavery). How are you redeeming the brief season of life you have as a parent? How can you make the most of the opportunities you have?

3. Finally, Paul says to not be foolish but to understand God's will and be filled with God's Spirit. What can you do to understand God's will for you as a Christian parent? Is there anything else that fills up your spirit that isn't God's will? What are you doing to let the Spirit of God fill you up?

Focus on Parenting
PLANS FOR NUMBERING YOUR CHILD'S DAYS

FROM THE LIFEGIVING PARENT, *CHAPTER 2*

If we fail to number our children's days—to be serious about how we will shape and influence their hearts and minds for God during our brief window of opportunity—then others will do that for us, with or without our consent. Our children will take from others— whether peers, culture, church, media, teachers, or strangers—the influence and instruction that God designed them to find primarily from us, their parents.

MAKE LIFEGIVING PLANS FOR YOUR FAMILY

You may be pretty good about numbering your own days, but what about numbering your children's days? You have a narrow window of opportunity to prepare each of your children for young adulthood and adulthood. That means you need to be prepared, as a disciple of Jesus, to do whatever it takes. Write down several ways that you can be redeeming your time to do God's will for your children. As a group, share and compare your ideas for numbering your children's days.

Engage with God

E

PRAYERS FOR NUMBERING YOUR CHILD'S DAYS

Share prayer requests related to the concepts you've discussed this week. Then move into a time of group prayer, letting these prompts direct you:

- ✳ Lord, teach us to number our days so that we can present to You hearts of wisdom.

- ✳ Jesus, let us be Your disciples who count the cost and finish the work of "building" our children.

- ✳ Help us to make the most of the season of childhood to do Your will for the sake of our children.

- ✳ Lord, life is too short to live foolishly, so show us how to be wise as Christian parents.

- ✳ Thank You, Lord, for Your Spirit within us that gives us Your life to give to our children.

NURTURING YOUR CHILD'S SPIRIT

Fathers, do not provoke your children to anger, but bring them up in the discipline and instruction of the Lord.

EPHESIANS 6:4, NASB

From The Lifegiving Parent, *chapter 3*

Nurture is the very essence of the lifegiving parenting this book is about—giving God's life to our children, feeding their spirits with the life of Christ from our own spirits. It's not just warm hugs, sweet words, and good feels—it is discipline and instruction, training and admonition. Nurture is hands-on and hands-around parenting. It cannot be done with a book, video, or new app. It doesn't happen by sending our children to Sunday school, Bible club, or camp. We cannot delegate nurture to another person or program. Only we as parents can nurture our children.

Thoughts on Nurturing Your Child's Spirit

If you want to be more lifegiving as a Christian parent, you will need to own the reality that God not only desires but also commands you to be a nurturing parent. Lifegiving is nurturing, and whether you're a mom or a dad, it's your parental and biblical duty. God has prewired your children's spirits to expect you to provide for their needs, and that includes the spiritual life of God that you have found and can give to them. This week's study will focus on God's design for you to nurture your children and some of the ways that nurture can be expressed.

Talking through L.I.F.E. Together

L *Listen to a Story*
A LIFEGIVING PARENTING MOMENT:

ABOUT SCREENS AND SPIRIT

The unplanned afternoon coffee break with Josh went mostly well for Molly. Talking about planning for the spiritual life of their family had left her feeling engaged with her husband and hopeful for the future, and yet also a bit fragmented and stressed. It was a free afternoon she originally had planned to use to work on her book. But plans change, and she always tried to be flexible for family. She also had a blog post due the next morning that she'd hoped to write, but now she would have to squeeze it in later that evening after the kids were in bed. And she would need to return calls that had gone to voice mail while she and Josh met. She closed her eyes and sighed.

That night after the younger kids were tucked in, Molly peeked in on Gracie, who could stay up later than her siblings. Through the crack in the open door, she could see Gracie with earbuds in, absorbed with something on her tablet. It had been a special twelfth birthday present from Josh, the family gadget master. Molly had felt a tinge of hesitancy, but Gracie was so excited, and Molly didn't want to disappoint her. She'd planned to create some guidelines for using it, but that never happened.

Molly lightly knocked on the door. When there was no response, she knocked again a bit harder. This time Gracie startled and looked over. Molly wondered if she saw in her daughter's sweet face a flash of teenage emotion, but she let it pass since her first child had always been such a good kid. However, her merciful moment was undone when Gracie then yanked out her earbuds with an audibly perturbed "What?" Molly thought to herself, *Oh no, Lord, not my Gracie. Not yet.*

"Hey, sweetheart, I just thought I'd stop and see if you wanted to talk before you went to bed. We haven't had much face time recently." She was trying to sound contemporary with the "face time" remark, but she knew it was a little lame. Still, Gracie would always talk with her.

"Oh, really? You mean, like . . . now? Can't we do it some other time? I mean, I love talking with you, but I wanted to see these new music videos right now. It's something I'm really interested in, and it's just what I do before bed."

Molly understood the appeal, but she wasn't thrilled that she didn't know what music Gracie was listening to, what music video site she was watching, or the fact that this had become a bedtime thing for her daughter. She just said, "Sure. That's fine. I'd love to hear more about your music." Molly felt like she was fumbling her attempt at engagement. "I mean what bands and artists you like these days. Well, good night, love."

Gracie tried to compensate for her earlier brush-off. "Sure. We can do that. Good night, Mom. Love you." And she put her earbuds back in and returned to her tablet.

Just like Josh had experienced his epiphany moment, this was Molly's. At first she felt she would be perfectly justified in being upset with her daughter, but it wasn't that easy. All she could see in her mind were all the times she had told Gracie she wasn't available to talk because she had to work on her book or blog. Or all the times she had just smiled at Gracie, turned from her phone, and whispered, "I really need to take this call." Now she was seeing herself mirrored in her sweet daughter. Gracie's attitude might not even be the dreaded spirit of "teenagerness" but just the acquired spirit of technological distraction. And it was Molly who was modeling it to her daughter! She closed her eyes and sighed, but this time with a heavy heart.

Molly did an unintentional facepalm but then decided it was appropriate. She prayed quietly that she wasn't too late to model the kind of face time that doesn't need a screen; to be more of a nurturing spirit in Gracie's life, not a neglectful one. But first, she thought, she needed to nurture her own spirit if she wanted to give real life—God's life—to her daughter. *Hope I'm not too late for me.*

- *Just for Fun:* Do you have any emerging teens in your house? Are there any new behaviors or attitudes you've had to respond differently to? Do the changes stem from how they are developing or from the way you are nurturing and modeling?

- How much do you think what you value and do affects your children? How do you model the use of gadgets and "screens" to your kids? How do you give them real face time?

I *Interact with the Word*
TRUTHS ABOUT NURTURING YOUR CHILD'S SPIRIT

EPHESIANS 6:1-4 | *Nurture your children in the Lord*

Children, obey your parents because you belong to the Lord, for this is the right thing to do. "Honor your father and mother." This is the first commandment with a promise: If you honor your father and mother, "things will go well for you, and you will have a long life on the earth." Fathers, do not provoke your children to anger by the way you treat them. Rather, bring them up with the discipline and instruction that comes from the Lord.

Word Notes: Paul's letter to the Ephesians includes what are often called "household codes." Though most of the letter's hearers were Jewish, many families living in non-Jewish areas such as Asia Minor held to a mixture of Jewish, Roman, and local pagan parenting practices. Paul's letters moved believers toward a Christian view of family and parenting. In these verses, he first speaks directly to children and then to fathers (or parents).

1. The primary responsibility God gives to children is to obey the fifth commandment. Why does Paul add "for this is the right thing to do"? Is he speaking to children or parents when he mentions the promise? How can you help your children learn to obey you? How do you expect them to honor you?

2. Paul commands fathers, literally, to "stop provoking" their children to anger, suggesting the children are angry because they're not receiving godly "discipline and instruction." How do you discipline your children in a way "that comes from the Lord"? How do you instruct them in the things of the Lord?

3. In the Greek, "bring them up" (*ektrepho*) literally means "to feed from" or "nurture." So Paul's command is to "nurture your children." How are discipline and instruction expressions of nurture? How does reading this verse with the word "nurture" change your understanding of what Paul is commanding you to do?

TITUS 2:11-14 | *Listening to the grace that nurtures*

The grace of God has been revealed, bringing
salvation to all people. And we are instructed to turn
from godless living and sinful pleasures. We should
live in this evil world with wisdom, righteousness,
and devotion to God, while we look forward with
hope to that wonderful day when the glory of our
great God and Savior, Jesus Christ, will be revealed.
He gave his life to free us from every kind of sin,
to cleanse us, and to make us his very own people,
totally committed to doing good deeds.

Word Notes: This passage is from one of Paul's "pastoral epistles" written directly to a person rather than to a church. In the longer part of this letter, Paul is giving instructions to the various groups within the body of Christ—older and younger men and women as well as servants. This passage comes after those instructions, putting them in a larger spiritual context. That context is relevant for parenting as well.

1. Paul personifies the biblical concept of grace, describing it as having appeared in order to teach us (vv. 11-12, NASB). The term he uses for "teach" often refers to the instruction or discipline of a child. In what ways or through what words is the influence of grace in your life as a Christian expressed to your children?

2. What Paul describes the Spirit doing in this passage is nurturing. Practically, how does grace teach you to turn from evil and turn to God? As a group, identify specific examples of "wisdom, righteousness, and devotion to God" in your lives as Christians. Then identify examples of those qualities in your lives as parents.

3. Paul puts these instructions in the context of the hope
   we have of Christ appearing, just as grace has appeared
   now. What tone and attitude does Paul express in these
   words? If you were to imitate him, how would that
   influence the way you nurture your children in godly
   living?

1 THESSALONIANS 2:10-12 | *Nurturing like Paul as a parent*

You yourselves are our witnesses—and so is God—
that we were devout and honest and faultless toward
all of you believers. And you know that we treated
each of you as a father treats his own children. We
pleaded with you, encouraged you, and urged you
to live your lives in a way that God would consider
worthy. For he called you to share in his Kingdom
and glory.

Word Notes: First Thessalonians is possibly Paul's earliest
recorded epistle, written after he had been with the believers
in Thessalonica for only about three weeks during his first
missionary journey. This passage is part of a longer section
in which Paul affirms his love and care for them using family
terms such as brothers, sisters, mother, children, and father.

The descriptive picture he paints of a father gives clues to his views of what nurture looks like.

1. Paul reminds the church of the nature of his pastoral relationship with them. As a parent, how does your nurturing relationship with your children reveal to them your devoutness, honesty, and blamelessness? Identify several specific actions and attitudes by which you can communicate each of those traits.

2. Paul reveals his own understanding of the kinds of qualities that he believes characterize a godly, nurturing father. Even if your children are young, in what ways can you plead with, encourage, and urge them to live to please God? How will that help to nurture their spirits and bring them the life of God?

3. Nurturing your children's spirits is not just about instructing them in how to lead a life pleasing to God. It is ultimately about helping them find themselves in the epic story God is writing of His Kingdom and glory. How are you nurturing your children's spirits

by introducing them to God's grand story of the Kingdom?

F · *Focus on Parenting*
PLANS FOR NURTURING YOUR CHILD'S SPIRIT

FROM THE LIFEGIVING PARENT, *CHAPTER 3*

You and your spouse are lifegiving parents together, bringing your children into engagement with the life of God in your home by nurturing their spirits. You both are feeding them from the life of God that is in your own spirits, and this is the life that will lead to their own relationships with God as they grow strong and healthy in Him. That's what lifegiving parents do.

MAKE LIFEGIVING PLANS FOR YOUR FAMILY

In the book, we focus on three parental practices for nurturing your child's spirit—training (discipline), instruction, and modeling. There are certainly many other ways to nurture, but these three are the relational priorities of nurturing discipleship. Below, list several things you can do to begin influencing your child in each of the three priorities. They don't have to be serious, just intentional. As a group, share and compare your ideas for nurturing your children's spirits.

E   *Engage with God*
PRAYERS FOR NURTURING YOUR CHILD'S SPIRIT

Share prayer requests related to the concepts you've discussed this week. Then move into a time of group prayer, letting these prompts direct you:

- Lord, give us hearts to learn and use the relational skills and priorities of nurturing.

- Help us not to exasperate or anger our children but to gently nurture them in You.

- Let us introduce our children to the grace of God that has instructed us as godly parents.

- Show our children, through us, their place in the wonderful story of Your eternal Kingdom.

- Help us to nurture our children "in the Lord" so they see Your life in ours and desire it for themselves.

GUARDING YOUR CHILD'S HEART

Guard your heart above all else, for it
determines the course of your life.

PROVERBS 4:23

From The Lifegiving Parent, *chapter 4*

When you guard your children's hearts so they let wisdom and
goodness in and keep folly and evil out, you not only direct them
into God's life but also set their courses on paths of righteousness.
It's all about helping them find and follow the life of God. That
is lifegiving parenting, and there may be nothing more impor-
tant for you as a lifegiving parent than guarding your children's
hearts.

Thoughts on Guarding Your Child's Heart

One of Sally's and my earliest realizations as new parents was
that we needed to guard our children's hearts. They had no

natural filters to determine which relationships, appetites, and influences would shape their hearts to please God and which ones would not. We were the gatekeepers for what would go into their hearts. Our intention was not to be legalistic or fearful about our gatekeeping role, but rather to be wise and positive. We made sure to let in the good—the biblical ideals of virtues and values—to shape our children's hearts for God. This week's study will explore how to be a lifegiving heart guarder.

Talking through L.I.F.E. Together

L | *Listen to a Story*
A LIFEGIVING PARENTING MOMENT:

ABOUT HEARTS AND APPETITES

"Hey, where is everybody?" Josh always enjoyed Saturday lunches with Molly and the kids. Today it was just Molly.

"The twins are playing next door. Gracie is at Brianna's. And the last time I saw T. J., he was in his room looking at your old comic books." Molly reported that last fact with a face that told Josh she wasn't really happy about it. She wasn't good at hiding feelings.

"Uh-huh. I see that face. Tell me what's bothering you. Something about my old comics?" Josh sat down with his turkey sandwich but waited for Molly to answer before picking it up.

"Do you remember that one of the things we talked about last weekend was protecting our kids' hearts—being careful about what they're reading, listening to, and watching?" Josh nodded and bit into his sandwich. "Well, I'm concerned about T. J. reading superhero comics this early. He's very young and impressionable right now." She sat down across from Josh. "It's not that the comics are bad or anything. I just think if he develops a taste for comics so early, he might not develop a taste for better reading." She looked at him with a serious face. "What would you think if we put the comics aside until he's older? I have some other ideas in mind." With that, she picked up her sandwich and took a bite.

Josh paused for a moment before responding. "You know what? I think that's a really good idea." Molly smiled. "David and T. J. spotted that box when we were organizing the storage room earlier. I just thought Dad's old comics would be a fun thing for them to look at. But now as I think about it, I didn't start reading those comics until I was almost twelve. My parents made sure before then that I had a great library so I would read good books." Josh pointed at his wife. "You're absolutely right. Six is too early to give T. J. an appetite for comics." He picked up the second half of his sandwich, held it up, and declared, "T. J. needs your good turkey sandwiches on organic whole wheat, not a bunch of baloney on white bread." Josh smiled and winked. "I'll talk to the boys, but go ahead and tell me what you have in mind."

Molly brightened up as she talked about creating a library of good, beautiful, and interesting illustrated storybooks that

T. J. could pull off the shelf and look at any time. She would read some classic books to the kids, like *Treasure Island* and The Chronicles of Narnia. She would get some audiobooks he and the twins could listen to. And they could have family reading nights when Josh would read aloud to everyone. It was just a start, and of course T. J. would see some comic books along the way, but she wanted to fill up his heart with good things. He would be a young teen before she knew it, so she wanted to use the time until then to train his appetites to value good and godly things. It was like building a fence in his heart to keep the good stuff in and the twaddle, as she called it, out.

Just then T. J. came in. "Hey, Dad. Your old superhero comics are really cool."

"Well, I always thought so, pal. I'm glad you got to see them. But I'm going to put them back in the storage room later. There will be another time you'll be able to enjoy them again. Until then, we'll be doing some new stuff your mom was telling me about." Josh lifted T. J. onto his lap while Molly brought another turkey sandwich to the table. "We're going to get you some good turkey sandwiches to read. Just like the ones your mom makes that you love so much."

T. J. looked at Josh and giggled. "You can't read a turkey sandwich! That's silly."

"Well, maybe it is, Tyler James McPherson. But you're going to love everything your mom feeds you to read. It will make you strong! It will protect your heart! You'll become a real superhero, ready to defend truth, goodness, beauty . . ."

T. J. crinkled his nose. "And the McPherson way! What do

you say?" T. J. smiled and nodded his head. "Well then, grab your sandwich and let's go read something good!"

- *Just for Fun:* What kinds of things are boxed in your storage areas that your children would enjoy finding? Did you read comic books as a kid? How old were you at the time? Who is your preferred superhero?

- How do you create appetites in a child for things that are good, beautiful, and true? How do you discourage appetites for things that might not be bad but prevent the best?

I *Interact with the Word*
TRUTHS ABOUT GUARDING YOUR CHILD'S HEART

PROVERBS 4:11-13, 18-19 | *Go straight on the path of life*

I will teach you wisdom's ways and lead you in straight paths. When you walk, you won't be held back; when you run, you won't stumble. Take hold of my instructions; don't let them go. Guard them, for they are the key to life. . . . The way of the righteous is like the first gleam of dawn, which shines ever brighter until the full light of day. But the way of the wicked is like total darkness. They have no idea what they are stumbling over.

Word Notes: In the first nine chapters of the book of Proverbs, Solomon is admonishing his sons to choose wisdom over folly as young men. He uses images of "the way of the righteous" and "the way of the wicked" to visualize the choice. The "path of life" is a common Hebraic metaphor alluded to here and used in several other places in Proverbs. It's the wisdom side of the binary choice we all face to follow God or not. It's a clear image children can understand.

1. Earlier (Proverbs 4:3-9) Solomon recalls his father, David, admonishing him as a child to hold on to his instruction, guard his heart, and be wise. Now (vv. 11-13) Solomon is doing the same with his sons. Did your parents do this for you? If so, share how it made you feel. If not, how can you do this for your child?

2. Solomon describes the "way [or path] of the righteous" (v. 18) as a road leading into a sunrise. What does he mean that it's "like the first gleam of dawn" that gets brighter until the full day? How has your understanding of God's righteousness been like a walk toward a sunrise?

3. We all will choose either to walk toward God into "full light" (v. 18) or to walk away from Him into "total darkness" (v. 19). How can you use the "path of life" metaphor to help your children visualize the Christian life? Discuss the words *direction*, *correction*, and *protection* and how they relate to your role as a path-of-life parent. (See pages 134–135 in *The Lifegiving Parent* for more detail.)

PROVERBS 4:23-27 | *Guard your heart for good and God*

Guard your heart above all else, for it determines
the course of your life. Avoid all perverse talk; stay
away from corrupt speech. Look straight ahead,
and fix your eyes on what lies before you. Mark
out a straight path for your feet; stay on the safe
path. Don't get sidetracked; keep your feet from
following evil.

Word Notes: Implicit in Solomon's admonition to "guard your heart" is not just the act of keeping bad things out but also letting good things in. Whatever goes into your children's hearts is what will determine their courses in life. The Hebrew word translated here as "course" suggests it will create the boundaries of their lives. That's why it's important "above all else" to stay on the straight and safe path of life and not be sidetracked by evil.

1. When Solomon admonishes his sons to "guard [their hearts] above all else," he's making it clear that the heart—the inner person that is the locus of the mind, emotions, and will—is where life's direction is determined. On a 1–10 scale, how serious are you about guarding your children's hearts? Where do you think you should be?

2. Solomon's warning against "perverse talk" and "corrupt speech" is not out of place in this passage. How might your words as a parent affect your heart? How might they affect your children's hearts? Jesus said our words reveal what is in our hearts (see Luke 6:45). How does that concept fit with Solomon's warning?

3. Jesus says that "the way is narrow that leads to life" (Matthew 7:14, NASB). For Solomon, what is it that "lies before" us that we need to "fix [our] eyes on" to stay on the path that leads to life? How can you help

your children understand that walking in God's way of life is both "straight" and "safe"?

PHILIPPIANS 4:8-9 | *Think about the ideals that really count*

And now, dear brothers and sisters, one final thing.
Fix your thoughts on what is true, and honorable,
and right, and pure, and lovely, and admirable.
Think about things that are excellent and worthy of
praise. Keep putting into practice all you learned and
received from me—everything you heard from me
and saw me doing. Then the God of peace will be
with you.

Word Notes: Paul enjoyed a close relationship with the believers in the Philippian church, whom he called partners in the gospel (see Philippians 1:5). As he closes his letter, his final admonition to them is to "think about" (fix their thoughts on) ideal values and virtues he had taught them that reflect God's goodness, and to put them into practice. If they do, the "God of peace" will be with them—a very lifegiving promise.

1. In his effort to encourage his Philippian friends to find the peace of God in their lives, Paul writes what is arguably one of his most specific statements about the ideals of the Christian faith that should most occupy our

minds. What are your initial feelings about so many ideals when reading this passage?

2. Paul first mentions six general values—truth, honor, righteousness, purity, loveliness, admirability. List several things you could think about that conform to each of those values. Then he refers to two "uber" values— excellence and praiseworthiness. List several things that help you think about each of those values.

3. This is a great list of values to consider as you think about guarding your children's hearts. From a negative perspective, how can these values help you keep out the bad stuff? From a positive one, how can they help you let in the good stuff? Talk about how you might teach your children to use these values as a filter.

Focus on Parenting
PLANS FOR GUARDING YOUR CHILD'S HEART

FROM THE LIFEGIVING PARENT, *CHAPTER 4*

As a lifegiving parent, you are the guardian and protector of your children's hearts, directing them away from "the way of the wicked" (Proverbs 4:19) and onto "the ancient paths, where the good way is" (Jeremiah 6:16, NASB). Your job as a heart guard is not complicated—it is to keep your children on God's "good way" and path of life so they will know and experience the very life of God in your home and family. That path is as old as the Bible's story and as new as the latest relationships, appetites, or influences looking for a place in your children's hearts.

MAKE LIFEGIVING PLANS FOR YOUR FAMILY

You guard your children's hearts not just to make sure they stay on the way of true life but also to make sure they'll know Jesus, who is "the way, the truth, and the life" (John 14:6). He is the embodiment of God's way of life. By guarding your children's hearts, you as lifegiving parents are giving them the life of Jesus. He is the source and end of every true and ideal virtue and value in Scripture. Write down some ways you can guard your children's hearts through protecting their relationships, appetites, and influences. As a group, share and compare your ideas for guarding your children's hearts.

E *Engage with God*

PRAYERS FOR GUARDING YOUR CHILD'S HEART

Share prayer requests related to the concepts you've discussed this week. Then move into a time of group prayer, letting these prompts direct you:

- Lord, give us a desire to guard our children's hearts from the bad and for the good.
- Be with us as we walk the path of life with our children and show them the way with You.
- Help us to guard what goes into our children's hearts that will set their course for life.
- Give us a vision for the ideal virtues and values that we need to let into our children's hearts.
- Lord, as we guard our children's hearts, let them see You as the way they must follow to find life.

RENEWING
YOUR CHILD'S MIND

Do not be conformed to this world, but be transformed by the renewing of your mind, so that you may prove what the will of God is, that which is good and acceptable and perfect.

ROMANS 12:2, NASB

From The Lifegiving Parent, *chapter 5*

Paul was not so concerned with the mind as an organ of human thinking and making the brain better so we don't waste our mental capabilities. Paul was concerned with our spiritual mind, the quality of our inner person that enables us to believe in Jesus, love and obey God, love others, understand biblical truth, assess error, resist sin and choose righteousness, and do God's will. He was concerned that we understand, strengthen, and renew "the mind of Christ" (1 Corinthians 2:16) that we have as believers. Why? Because that is where the life of Christ is found—the life within us.

Thoughts on Renewing Your Child's Mind

"You are what you think" is not a Bible verse, but it is a Bible truth. The book of Proverbs teaches that the way you think about life makes you either wise or a fool—it's all in your mind. The New Testament teaches that we have a mind set either on the flesh or on the Spirit, a worldly mind or the "mind of Christ" (1 Corinthians 2:16). The spiritual mind is not static but dynamic; it must be "renewed" by the Spirit with God's grace and truth (John 1:17, NASB). Your mind as a parent must be renewed by God so you have His life to give to your children. Your children's minds must be renewed so they are able to respond to God.

Talking through L.I.F.E. Together

L | *Listen to a Story*
A LIFEGIVING PARENTING MOMENT:

ABOUT MINDS AND MORE

The McPherson family came out of church together into a glorious fall day. Josh and Molly greeted Pastor Goodson at the door and then visited with friends, purposely giving their kids some time to expend pent-up energy. The older ones engaged in a noisy game of tag with other children while T. J. enjoyed the swings and slide on the playground. But with a familiar whistle from their dad, they were soon all in the van on their way to Sunday lunch.

"So, what did you kids think about the sermon?" Josh never tired of his postchurch discussions. He believed they encouraged his children to listen, think about what they were hearing, and be ready to express an opinion in a family discussion. It was his version of Sunday schooling. "What did the pastor say the two commands of Romans 12:2 are? Who remembers?"

David, who had fallen asleep in church last Sunday, was first to respond this week. "Pastor said the verse says to 'stop the world' and 'go to the Word.'" He looked proud that he knew the answer. "He said it was like traffic signs. Stop and Go."

"Davey scores!" That was Josh's nickname for David since "Davey and Amy" went together so well. "You were really listening well, Son. Way to go. Get it? Go?" All the kids groaned. "Somebody else, then—what did he mean by 'Stop the world'?"

Not to be outdone by her twin brother, Amy was next to answer. "Pastor said it meant that we should stop letting the world tell us what to think. I think he meant that a lot of the world doesn't think like God, so we shouldn't listen to it."

"And Amy scores! You guys are amazing." The conversation went on with everyone getting in some points. Davey wanted to know what a Go sign was, but no one had a good answer other than that it must be green and say "Go." These times in the car were never like a quiz but more like a fun game show. The conversations kept going even as they got to the restaurant.

Later, after eating lunch, Josh and Molly talked at the table while the kids ate their free mini-cones of soft-serve ice cream. Molly wondered out loud if they were doing enough to "stop the world" from affecting how their kids thought. She wasn't paranoid and hadn't seen any signs of what Pastor Goodson called "worldly thinking," but she just felt there were so many worldly messages everywhere these days. How in the world could they stop all of them from getting in their kids' heads?

Josh shook his head. "We can't. There's no way. It's going to get in—it just is. And our kids will have to live in the world with all that worldly thinking going on. That's why I think the best defense is a strong offense. As Pastor Goodson said, we can't avoid hearing *what* the world thinks, but we can stop it from telling us *how* to think. *That's* our choice. And the way to do that is to go to the Word so we know how God wants us to think."

"Maybe you're right." Molly nodded her agreement. "So then, Coach McPherson, what's your big play? Just what do you want our offensive line to do? How do we keep our team scoring? Make your call, big guy." She was being playful, but inside she was also serious.

Josh took the challenge. "We just keep playing our best game. That's all. But we play harder, and we play stronger. We never give up. We only give more." He was in his locker room pep talk mode now. "More dinner table discussions about our faith. More thoughtful family nights. More consistent family devotions. More stories about faithful Christians. More ministry to others. More Bible. More talk. More walk. We're in it to win it. It's more for the score!"

When Josh finished, he looked up to see five sets of eyes staring at him. Everyone was perfectly still. T. J. grinned and broke the silence with "Daddy scores!" The rest is family history, the kind that gets retold and embellished through the years. A T-shirt with "More for the score!" emblazoned on it showed up at Christmas. It was more for the win.

- *Just for Fun:* Describe your family as a football team. Who's the quarterback? Who's best at running? Who's best at catching? Who's a cheerleader? What is your team name and mascot?

- What do you think about Josh's "more" offensive strategy? When it comes to "stop the world," are you more reactive or proactive? How can you "go to the Word" more often in your family?

I | *Interact with the Word*
TRUTHS ABOUT RENEWING YOUR CHILD'S MIND

ROMANS 12:1-2 | *The transformation of a renewed mind*

Dear brothers and sisters, I plead with you to give your bodies to God because of all he has done for you. Let them be a living and holy sacrifice—the kind he will find acceptable. This is truly the way to worship him. Don't copy the behavior and customs of this world, but let God transform you into a new person by changing the way you think. Then you will learn to know God's will for you, which is good and pleasing and perfect.

Word Notes: These two verses in the book of Romans are a hinge between looking back on God's work for us in chapters 1–11 (v. 1) and looking forward to our walk with God in chapters 12–16 (v. 2). It is, in some ways, Paul's succinct way of saying what it means to be a disciple of Christ—to worship Him and to be transformed by Him. Paul says that is how we can show that God's will is authentic.

1. In verse 1, Paul looks back on all God has done and says that the reasonable, or logical, response is to worship Him as a living sacrifice. When you consider all God has done for you, what is your response? What does it mean to be a "living sacrifice"? How do you as a family look back on God's work?

2. In verse 2, Paul looks ahead at how to live. The first thing he says is to stop letting this time you live in, or "this world," tell you how to think (the word for "world," *aiōn*, means an "age"). How do you resist letting your

mind be shaped by modern "isms" and philosophies? How do you protect your children from them?

3. Next, Paul says you need to be transformed by changing the way you think, or literally by "the renewing of your mind" (NASB). What are you doing that continuously renews your mind? How much is God's Word part of that renewal? What are you doing to renew your children's minds?

EPHESIANS 4:21-24 | *The new nature of a renewed mind*

Since you have heard about Jesus and have learned the truth that comes from him, throw off your old sinful nature and your former way of life, which is corrupted by lust and deception. Instead, let the Spirit renew your thoughts and attitudes. Put on your new nature, created to be like God—truly righteous and holy.

Word Notes: Paul's magisterial letter to the Ephesians, following the same pattern as his letter to the church in Rome, moves from Christian theology in chapters 1–3 (being "seated" with Christ in heaven) to Christian living in chapters 4–6 ("walking" with Christ on earth). This passage is about the role of the mind in moving from what we once were to what we now are in Christ.

1. Paul invites his readers, since they know Jesus and His teachings, to "throw off" their sin natures. They are believers, but they're still living in their old ways. As a Christian, how do you sometimes have to reject the pull to your old-nature way of living? What is the role of your mind in that process?

2. Paul says the Ephesians should "be renewed in the spirit of [their] mind[s]" (v. 23, NASB). He admonishes them that the path to laying aside their sin natures is changing how they think—it all begins in the mind. How have you experienced that kind of mind renewal? In what areas of parenting have you seen that change?

3. Finally, Paul says the believers should then "put on
    [their] new nature" made in the likeness of God. The
    renewing of the mind directs the whole process of
    laying aside the old and putting on the new. How do
    you keep your mind renewed by God? How would you
    explain that renewing process to your children?

2 CORINTHIANS 10:4-5 | *Capturing thoughts that won't obey*

We use God's mighty weapons, not worldly weapons,
to knock down the strongholds of human reasoning
and to destroy false arguments. We destroy every
proud obstacle that keeps people from knowing
God. We capture their rebellious thoughts and teach
them to obey Christ.

Word Notes: This letter was written not long after the first
letter to the Corinthians, but the tone and range of emotions are much different. Problems and issues still infect
the church, but now Paul is having to respond to criti-
cisms about his authority and integrity. In this passage, he
forcefully asserts his authority to confront false and deceit-
ful teaching that is dividing the body and challenging his
ministry.

1. Paul says we need spiritual weapons for spiritual battles, weapons that will knock down mental "strongholds" and "false arguments." How do people build "strongholds" around false ideas in their minds? What are God's weapons for knocking down those strongholds? How can a Christian guard against strongholds?

2. The mind is clearly the battleground for the soul. Paul confronts false teachings that keep others from knowing God, and he talks about taking thoughts captive to make them submit to Christ. How can we do that in our own minds? How do you take a thought captive? How do you make it "obey Christ"?

3. Though Paul's focus may be on nonbelievers and false teachers, he describes a mental process that Christians, too, can use. Taking wrong thinking captive must precede renewing the mind. What kinds of thoughts might need to be made captive? How can we help our children do this as well?

F *Focus on Parenting*
PLANS FOR RENEWING YOUR CHILD'S MIND

FROM THE LIFEGIVING PARENT, *CHAPTER 5*

Of all the heartbeats of lifegiving parenting, this one—renewing your children's minds—arguably requires the most from you as the parent. Your children, whether they are young and immature or beginning to mature as young teens, will be looking to you not just to understand what it means to have a redeemed mind but also to see what it means to live out of a redeemed mind. You are living out the spirit of Paul's admonition for them: "Follow my example, as I follow the example of Christ" (1 Corinthians 11:1, NIV). In many ways, your mature example of having a redeemed mind will serve as their first opportunity to practice what it means to be a disciple of Christ—to follow the way of God and do His will.

MAKE LIFEGIVING PLANS FOR YOUR FAMILY

This heartbeat of lifegiving parenting cuts both ways—you cannot renew your child's mind if your mind is not renewed; you cannot keep the isms of this age out of your child's mind if they're in your own. See top of page 62. Under "Keeping Out," identify ways you can protect your and your children's minds from the isms of this age. Under "Letting In," identify ways to renew your and your children's minds with God's truth. As a group, share and compare your ideas for renewing your children's minds.

• *Keeping Out*

• *Letting In*

E *Engage with God*
PRAYERS FOR RENEWING YOUR CHILD'S MIND

Share prayer requests related to the concepts you've discussed this week. Then move into a time of group prayer, letting these prompts direct you:

※ Lord, give us hearts for renewing our children's minds with the truth of Your Word.

※ Even as our children are young, let Your Word begin the work of transformation in them.

※ Help us to lay aside our old selves and put on our new selves as parents.

※ Teach us how to take our thoughts captive for Christ and how to help our children do that as well.

※ Help us to protect our minds, and our children's minds, from the bad and turn them toward the good.

STRENGTHENING YOUR CHILD'S FAITH

Jesus said, "Let the children alone, and do not hinder them from coming to Me; for the kingdom of heaven belongs to such as these."

MATTHEW 19:14, NASB

From The Lifegiving Parent, *chapter 6*

Giving your children a stronger faith is not just about having them memorize Scriptures, read Christian books, or do Bible lessons. It is ultimately about your showing them the abundant life of God through your own faith life and showing that you are diligent to grow in all the godly virtues that come out of your faith. None of us will ever exhibit all those virtues perfectly, but your children will see you making faith your priority, trusting God to transform your life, and depending on Him when you falter. It's not about having "arrived" but about walking daily with God. You can teach your children what Scripture says about faith and belief, but they will learn best about the reality of faith when it is lived out before their eyes in your life. That is lifegiving parenting.

Thoughts on Strengthening Your Child's Faith

For most people, the simplest definition of *faith* is what you believe about God. But someone can believe almost anything about God and be called "a person of faith." Christian faith, by contrast, is all about Jesus Christ—His birth, life, death, resurrection, church, and Kingdom. Faith in the person, work, and teaching of Jesus is the only lifegiving faith there is. That is the faith we as Christian parents want to strengthen in our children. Not just a childish faith that comes only from knowing simple Bible stories, but faith that Jesus is who He said He is and that He's alive and living inside us. That's the living faith we have to give them—the life of God in us.

Talking through L.I.F.E. Together

Listen to a Story

A LIFEGIVING PARENTING MOMENT:

ABOUT FAITH AND FROYO

Traditions are highly valued in the McPherson family. One of the most revered is the DNO. Dad Night Out is a one-on-one dinner with Dad at a restaurant of the child's choice, typically followed by a stop at Fogurty's Frozen Yogurt Shoppe before heading back home. All the kids take their dad's humor in stride when Josh makes sure to remind each child that Fogurty's is the real reason he does DNOs. "They say Fogurty's will make a believer out of you. I didn't know it was that simple: Eat froyo; become a believer. That's the way it ought to be." They all groan on cue.

Except for Gracie tonight. She seemed quiet and distant, so Josh held back on the dad humor. The RBH project had knocked him off his usual rhythms, and it had been several months since he had tagged Gracie for a DNO. He had always taken special delight in these nights with his first child. Tonight she'd picked La Marianne's, a family favorite French coffee shop and eatery, but her heart just didn't seem in it. Josh was surprised by how much she had grown up over the summer. While he was working, she was transforming from cute little girl to lovely young woman. He wasn't feeling very confident that she would let him into her inner world tonight, but he would try. He prayed quietly as he parked the SUV.

Dinner was all small talk, family stories, and polite conversation. As they were finishing their drinks, Josh decided to be more direct. He carefully asked gently probing questions about what Gracie was going through as she approached young adulthood. Her sudden openness caught him off guard. "Dad, did you ever have doubts about God and Christianity? I mean, did you ever wonder if it was all just a made-up story?" He hadn't seen that coming, but he didn't react. He just kept talking, asking questions, listening. Their cups had long since gone dry, so he said, "I know you may not feel like going to Fogurty's tonight, but I'd really like us to go there to finish this conversation. Is that all right?" Despite Gracie's clouded feelings, she would *never* forgo the stop at Fogurty's. She nodded and they left.

With self-serve containers in hand, filled with a variety of froyo flavors and toppings, they sat down at a secluded table outside. Josh jumped right in. He let Gracie know that doubt was natural and nothing to be ashamed about. "In fact," he said, "it takes a lot of faith to doubt well. If you didn't doubt your faith at all, then you'd be either an unbeliever or just brainwashed." He hoped she understood what he meant. "Doubt is a sure sign that your faith is alive, that you're 'working out your salvation.'" He was pretty sure she knew that verse. "The deal is, from what I'm hearing, you're just doubting your faith, you're not putting faith in your doubt. There's a big difference."

Josh pointed to his many-colored cup of froyo flavors. "I may doubt that I'll like every one of these flavors, but I won't know until I taste them. The more I taste them, the more I can believe that I will like them." He took a bite and over-dramatized his positive reaction. "Look, I know this is lame, but I'm your dad, so go with me. Faith is like froyo. There are lots of flavors, and you have to taste them to know whether or not you'll believe in them. It's not all at once but a little at a time. Right now, you're just beginning to get tastes of real faith, of adult faith. And that's good. Keep tasting. Give God a chance to show you that He's worth believing in. Does any of that make sense?" Josh shut up and waited.

Gracie poked at her yogurt, then looked up at Josh with a blank face. "Yeah, Dad, you're right. That was pretty lame." She paused with a wry smile that made Josh grin. "But that actually does make sense. I really appreciate your drawing me out tonight and wanting to help. I'll think about all you said."

Josh couldn't keep it in. "Wow! So it is true. Fogurty's really can make a believer out of you! I knew it all along." And with that, Gracie couldn't help but let out a big, laughing groan.

- *Just for Fun:* What are your family's special traditions? If you were to adopt a DNO in your family, what would it include? What are your kids' favorite eateries? What is your Fogurty's equivalent?

- How would you respond to children who expressed doubts about their faith? What kinds of questions would you ask them? How would you help them "work out" their salvation?

I *Interact with the Word*
TRUTHS ABOUT STRENGTHENING YOUR CHILD'S FAITH

MATTHEW 18:2-6 | *Little ones who believe in Jesus*

Jesus called a little child to him and put the child among them. Then he said, "I tell you the truth, unless you turn from your sins and become like little children, you will never get into the Kingdom of Heaven. So anyone who becomes as humble as this little child is the greatest in the Kingdom of Heaven. And anyone who welcomes a little child like this on my behalf is welcoming me. But if you cause one of these little ones who trusts in me to fall into sin, it would be better for you to have a large millstone tied around your neck and be drowned in the depths of the sea."

Word Notes: Jesus and the disciples are in Capernaum, on the shore of the Galilean sea. Jesus had preached, healed, and called disciples here. It was home for Him. He and the disciples have just come down from a nearby mountain, where Jesus had been transfigured. The disciples now are arguing and ask Jesus, "Who is greatest in the Kingdom of Heaven?" (v. 1). Jesus uses the question to teach His disciples a lesson of faith.

1.   Jesus calls a young child, maybe five years old, to come to Him. His answer to the disciples' question is shocking—become like a child or forget the Kingdom. If you had been there, how might you have responded? What would you think if it had been your child with Jesus?

2.   Jesus answers the question about who would be greatest in the Kingdom—whoever "becomes as humble," or as lowly, as the child. What do you imagine the disciples thought about that? A child had no standing in Jewish

law or society, so the disciples must have been surprised that they would have to "become" that low. What is Jesus saying?

3. Then Jesus gets even more radical—He elevates a child's faith by using the same Greek word for adult belief when he refers to "one of these little ones who trusts [or *believes*] in me." A child's faith is just as real as the disciples'! How does the way you think about your child's faith compare with Jesus' way?

ROMANS 1:16-17 | *Faith in Christ is the source of life*

I am not ashamed of this Good News about Christ. It is the power of God at work, saving everyone who believes—the Jew first and also the Gentile. This Good News tells us how God makes us right in his sight. This is accomplished from start to finish by faith. As the Scriptures say, "It is through faith that a righteous person has life."

Word Notes: Paul greets the Roman church, letting them know that he is eager to preach the gospel to them. These two verses (16-17) mark the beginning of his lengthy theological defense of the gospel in chapters 1–11, which begins with his teaching about how our sin separates us from God. This passage is like a minipreamble. These two simple verses are faith challenging if we let them be.

1. Why does Paul start off saying he is "not ashamed" of the gospel, the "Good News about Christ"? Is that something you are comfortable saying publicly? Why or why not? Do you think your children would understand from your life that you're not ashamed of the gospel, that you are confident in it and vocal about it?

2. The gospel saves everyone who believes—who has faith—whether they are a Jew like Paul was or a Gentile like many of us. Even if you believe everyone can be saved, do you ever find that difficult to live out in real life? If so, how? What would your children say about your "everyone" faith?

3. Salvation is accomplished only and completely by faith (v. 17), not by works or anything else. The person who

is considered righteous because of faith in Christ has life. It's easy to believe that going to church or doing good things is what saves us, rather than having faith in Christ. How can you guard against that error as a parent? If asked, what might your children say about how people can be saved?

HEBREWS 11:1, 6 | *Faith is the assurance of our hope*

Faith shows the reality of what we hope for; it is the evidence of things we cannot see. . . . And it is impossible to please God without faith. Anyone who wants to come to him must believe that God exists and that he rewards those who sincerely seek him.

Word Notes: These are a few of the introductory remarks to the grand "Hall of Faith" passage in the book of Hebrews, a long list of Old Testament saints who lived and died "by faith." It is a remarkable testimony and affirmation of the faith of those who followed God, often into martyrdom in His name, long before Christ appeared—all because they believed God would keep His promises.

1. We don't "hope" for something we can see, but "faith" gives assurance and evidence that our hope is not just wishing. How do you find that faith, your belief in

God, gives you confidence in your hope of heaven? How can you strengthen your child's faith to create a confident hope in God's promises?

2. Faith is the key to pleasing God, but you "must believe" that He exists and that He rewards those who diligently seek Him. Why does faith that is pleasing to God require both of those beliefs? How are you teaching your child to have a faith that will please God? How do you "sincerely seek him"?

3. As parents, we should strengthen our children's faith by aiming at these verses in Hebrews. They point to a faith that is confident that God is going to be the kind of God He says He is and that He will do what He promises to do. How can you talk about and model this kind of faith at home to strengthen your child's faith?

Focus on Parenting
PLANS FOR STRENGTHENING YOUR CHILD'S FAITH

FROM THE LIFEGIVING PARENT, *CHAPTER 6*

God sees a valid and even vibrant faith in children of all ages—in your children! As lifegiving parents, make it your commitment to look for that faith in your children, acknowledging and affirming it whenever you can. It probably won't sound like adult faith, and that's as it should be. It's an innocent and seedling kind of faith that should be watered, cultivated, and tended. It's possible you'll be tempted to correct its immature or misdirected expressions or, perhaps worse, to just ignore it; but resist either urge. Instead, engage your children's faith and draw it out.

MAKE LIFEGIVING PLANS FOR YOUR FAMILY

Full faith, or belief, is an abstract concept that doesn't fully form in a child until puberty and beyond. But according to Jesus, even the nascent and forming faith of a child is real and valid, so it can be affirmed and strengthened. It is like a spiritual muscle that will get stronger with use. Identify below some practical ways that you can exercise and strengthen your child's faith at home. As a group, share and compare your ideas for strengthening your children's faith.

Engage with God
PRAYERS FOR STRENGTHENING YOUR CHILD'S FAITH

Share prayer requests related to the concepts you've discussed this week. Then move into a time of group prayer, letting these prompts direct you:

❋ Lord, give us eyes to see, affirm, and strengthen the forming faith of our children.

❋ Let us see our children through the eyes of the Savior, who believed in the faith of children.

❋ Give us, by Your Spirit, an unwavering confidence in the gospel of Christ that saves by faith.

❋ Strengthen our faith as parents, that we may please You and show Your reality to our children.

❋ Strengthen our confidence, that we may be parents who strengthen the faith of our children.

SHAPING YOUR CHILD'S WILL

All Scripture is inspired by God and is useful to teach us what is true and to make us realize what is wrong in our lives. It corrects us when we are wrong and teaches us to do what is right.

2 TIMOTHY 3:16

From The Lifegiving Parent, *chapter 7*

Our children, like all humans, have many desires, drives, intentions, and loves that are neutral in and of themselves but can become good or bad depending on how we shape their wills and what they will to choose and pursue. It's all the work of what Scripture calls the soul, the inner person of the heart that is the locus of the mind, emotions, and will. Those three qualities of the soul all work together in the act of making choices, and yet the will alone translates thoughts and feelings into decisions. The will reveals who you are by what you choose and do.

Thoughts on Shaping Your Child's Will

All parents know their child has a will from that first defiant "No!" It is that developing will, trained and shaped by you in childhood, that ultimately will determine the person your child becomes. We are all, in some way, the product of our choices in life, and especially the choice of whether or not we follow the path of life with God. Shaping your children's wills as a lifegiving parent is about influencing them to choose to do the will of God. That's what makes it lifegiving—you are connecting your children with the heart of the living God. This week's study will explore the shaping of your children's developing wills for Him.

Talking through L.I.F.E. Together

L *Listen to a Story*
A LIFEGIVING PARENTING MOMENT:

ABOUT WILL AND WORK

Home at Last Builders, Josh's custom home business, has grown steadily since he started it ten years ago. When he was building their own home at the same time, he included in the plans a large storage room off the back of their garage. He used it both for family and for business. Even with the separate work office he opened a few years later, "Shedzilla," as he calls the room, is still full of his building tools and supplies. He's an organized type, but he has to be diligent to keep the space from succumbing to the ravages of stuff and clutter. To give the boys a little training in the manly duties of garage and yard maintenance, and more importantly to

create some time to be with them as a dad, Josh periodi-
cally enlists them to help organize and clean Shedzilla—the
monster that, he says, "can be depleted but will never be
completely defeated."

They were doing battle the day they found the comic
books. Just before the discovery, Josh had given Davey a
mildly tedious but simple task—taking screws, nuts and
bolts, and nails from a catchall can that had been filling
up for years and organizing them into three drawers. "This
is your personal task, Davey. If you get started today and
keep doing it until it's done, then we'll go get a blended
froyo at Fogurty's. How does that sound?" Davey smiled
and nodded unconvincingly, then slowly started separating
pieces on the workbench where Josh had poured out some
of the can. But soon T. J. found the comics box and noisily
called to Davey, and that was the end of battling Shedzilla
for that Saturday.

Diligence was not always Davey's strong suit, so Josh knew
he might need some help. A few days later, Josh reminded
him about the job. He was much more concerned about
training and shaping Davey's developing will to work than he
was about the actual work this little job would require. "Hey,
Davey. How's the taming of the screws coming along?" Josh
smiled; Davey obviously didn't get it. "Well, never mind.
Why don't you plan to spend an hour in Shedzilla some day
this week, working on your project? I think you might even
get it finished if you do."

Davey stopped on the stairs coming down from his room.
"Dad," he said, looking down at the floor, "I want to do my

job, and I will, but I don't like it when I'm out there all alone. It makes me feel sort of, like, sad." He looked up at Josh. "I can do it, but it's hard. Not the organizing, but the doing it alone. Could I ask Amy or T. J. to come be with me while I work on it?"

Josh was proud of what he was hearing. Davey wasn't being willfully resistant about doing the job. He was just trying to express what his emerging nine-year-old personality was like. He preferred working *with* people, not alone. He was a "people and team" kind of guy. Josh was definitely more the independent type when it came to work, but he understood Davey and didn't want to project his own personality onto him. He'd been learning about the differences in personalities at his business to help his employees understand each other better. He also wanted to understand himself better as an employer—and now, he also realized, as a dad.

"Davey, I think I understand what you're saying, and I'm really proud of your willingness to be diligent." They sat down together on the stairs. "How about this? Saturday morning, you and me in Shedzilla together. We'll be a team—get some iced tea, put on your favorite music, and together we'll tame the screws, the nuts and bolts, and the nails, just like a fine-tuned Shakespearean play." He knew that would also go unappreciated, but he had to say it anyway. "I'd like to be the one who gets to work with you. Would that be okay?"

That Saturday, Davey and his dad tag-teamed and tamed the task in less than an hour. They talked and laughed, and Davey told his dad about stories and poems he was writing, something Josh realized he might not have heard about without this time together. Shedzilla wasn't going away, but they had successfully depleted one small part of the monster. And that deserved a trip to Fogurty's.

- *Just for Fun:* How are your children's personalities different? Do you have team workers and solo workers? Organizers and unorganizers? Extroverts and introverts? Relational and rational types?

- What do you think are the most effective ways to shape and train a child's will? What happens when you create tasks and expect obedience no matter what? What do you find are the relational aspects to will shaping?

I *Interact with the Word*
TRUTHS ABOUT SHAPING YOUR CHILD'S WILL

COLOSSIANS 3:20-21 | *Household codes for kids and dads*

Children, always obey your parents, for this pleases the Lord. Fathers, do not aggravate your children, or they will become discouraged.

Word Notes: There is nothing recorded in Scripture to indicate that Paul ever visited the Colossian church. The believers there were mostly Gentiles (non-Jews), and Paul writes primarily to confront an unnamed heresy, probably about the nature of Christ. But he also instructs them in Christian

79

basics, such as relationships and "household codes." In this passage, he is addressing children and fathers.

1. Although he doesn't quote the fifth commandment to "honor" parents, Paul clearly alludes to it when he commands children to "obey" them. If honoring is about attitude and obeying is about actions, which is your child better at? Which are you better at training? Which is more about the will?

2. Paul addresses the children directly with an imperative (a command), which can literally mean "keep on obeying," suggesting both an action and an attitude. How do you help your child learn to obey as a habit and to keep an attitude of obedience that "pleases the Lord"? What is your best will-training approach?

3. Fathers can often become harsh to make children obey. Paul commands them to stop provoking their children to anger, which can leave them dispirited. Is this something you (dads) sometimes do to your children? How do you think dispirited children's wills respond to train-

ing? How can you train children's wills to obey without breaking their spirits?

2 TIMOTHY 3:16-17 | *How inspired Scripture trains the will*

All Scripture is inspired by God and is useful to teach us what is true and to make us realize what is wrong in our lives. It corrects us when we are wrong and teaches us to do what is right. God uses it to prepare and equip his people to do every good work.

Word Notes: The last recorded letter of Paul was written to his "son in the faith" and ministry protégé, Timothy. Paul wrote from Rome, awaiting his fate from the emperor Nero while in chains in a cold dungeon. He wrote to Timothy both to encourage him personally and to strengthen the church through him. This passage would help establish the role of Scripture as the focus of worship and instruction in the church.

1. All Scripture, old and new, is inspired—God breathed (*theopneustos*). God speaks through His Word. And, Paul says, it is "useful," or profitable—it accomplishes what it intends. Will training must begin with God's

will. How are you integrating God's Word and will into your home and family life?

2. Paul asserts that God's inspired Word is useful for four specific purposes: teaching, reproving, correcting, and training. How do you express those purposes in your use of the Bible at home? What seems to work best? How are you training your child to "do what is right" from God's Word?

3. *Prepare* can also mean "to train." In what ways has your knowledge of Scripture prepared or trained you for parenting? How has it equipped you to do God's "good work" as a parent? How are you using Scripture to prepare and equip your child to grow up "to do every good work"?

PSALM 143:8-10 | *God has a will for you*

Let me hear of your unfailing love each morning, for
I am trusting you. Show me where to walk, for I give
myself to you. Rescue me from my enemies, LORD;
I run to you to hide me. Teach me to do your will,
for you are my God. May your gracious Spirit lead
me forward on a firm footing.

Word Notes: Psalm 143 is the last of the seven penitential
psalms, or psalms of confession for sorrow or sin (6, 32, 38,
51, 102, 130, 143). The first half (vv. 1-6) is David's appeal
to God about his distress; the second half (vv. 7-12) is his
prayer to God for help. This portion of the psalm is notable for
David's request that God would teach him. His need is not just
for God to intervene but also for him to learn to do God's will.

1. David begins verse 8 by acknowledging God's faithful
    love and declaring his trust in God even in the midst
    of trouble. When "enemies" (real or metaphorical) at-
    tack your family, what is your first response? Does your
    child hear and see you trusting God and affirming His
    faithful love? How is that important for shaping your
    child's will?

2. David submits himself to and takes refuge in God,
    praying for direction and protection. He was a man
    of battle, but here he surrenders his situation to God.
    Have you ever felt helpless in the face of difficult cir-
    cumstances? How did your children see you respond to
    God? What choices of will did they observe?

3. Finally David prays, "Teach me to do your will." He
    is asking for personal guidance so he can find "firm
    footing" for his life. Describe a time when you needed
    specific guidance from God. How did the Spirit of God
    answer your need? How can you shape your child's will
    to choose to trust God in this way?

F *Focus on Parenting*
PLANS FOR SHAPING YOUR CHILD'S WILL

FROM THE LIFEGIVING PARENT, *CHAPTER 7*

*Shaping your children's wills to want to obey God is one of the
most challenging tasks you will encounter as a lifegiving parent. The fruit of your influence will be in direct proportion to
the amount of time you can invest engaging in your children's*

lives physically, mentally, emotionally, and spiritually. It will be one of your most demanding responsibilities as a parent and yet one with arguably the greatest rewards. Who your children become as adults will, in many ways, be determined by how you influence and shape their wills now as children—they will become products of the choices they make in childhood and youth, whether good or bad, on your watch. God's path of life is all about choices, and you're shaping your children's wills to choose to stay on that path.

MAKE LIFEGIVING PLANS FOR YOUR FAMILY

James calls the tongue a "restless evil" that cannot be tamed, with which we bless God and curse men (see James 3:8, NASB). And yet . . . the tongue is controlled by the will. An untrained will is the real restless evil. Perhaps the will can never be completely tamed, but it can be trained and shaped to choose to follow God and do His will. List below some ways that you can make shaping your children's developing wills a higher priority. As a group, share and compare your ideas for shaping your children's wills.

E *Engage with God*
PRAYERS FOR SHAPING YOUR CHILD'S WILL

Share prayer requests related to the concepts you've discussed this week. Then move into a time of group prayer, letting these prompts direct you:

❊ Lord, teach us how to control our wills so that we can shape our children's wills for You.

❊ Help us to model self-control so we can help our children honor and obey us.

❊ Show us how to use Your Word to prepare and equip our children to do Your work.

❊ Lord, let our children see us learning to trust You and do Your will so they can too.

❊ Give us wisdom, God, to shape our children's wills to choose to follow and do Your will.

CULTIVATING YOUR CHILD'S CHARACTER

*The seed in the good soil, these are the ones who have
heard the word in an honest and good heart, and
hold it fast, and bear fruit with perseverance.*

LUKE 8:15, NASB

From The Lifegiving Parent, *chapter 8*

*If your children learn godly character qualities from you during
childhood, they will simply continue walking in them whenever
they accept Jesus as their Savior. The good and godly character you cultivate in them as children will create the "good soil"
in their hearts that will at some point become the character
of Christ when they become "new creatures" in Him and the
Holy Spirit begins working in them (see Galatians 5:22-23;
Colossians 3:12-15). Cultivating good character in your children now will keep them on the way of life with God, which
will lead them to Jesus, who is "the way, even the truth and the
life" (translators' note, John 14:6, NET©).*

Thoughts on Cultivating Your Child's Character

Christian character is not just an accumulation of discrete character traits. That's behaviorism, the idea that your children come into the world as blank slates and you control what they will become. Your children are whole people whose spirits are designed by God to look to you for what it means to become a good human. Through training, instruction, and modeling, you help them become what God intended them to be. You create good soil in their hearts so good character can grow there until Christ comes in and makes them new creatures. Character is a deep well of study. We can only scratch the surface this week.

Talking through L.I.F.E. Together

L | *Listen to a Story*
A LIFEGIVING PARENTING MOMENT:

ABOUT TEA AND CHARACTER

Molly was never one to pass up an opportunity to spend special time with one of her daughters. There were just too many cozy nooks and bay window seats in her home to let them go to waste. So when Josh set aside a couple of hours to work with Davey in Shedzilla, she immediately invited Amy to a private tea-and-talk time with her, or what she liked to call a "special-tea." She would go all out with the bone china tea set, silver, candles, flowers, and pleasant music. Then she would serve the family's favorite English tea with fresh scones, clotted cream, and strawberry jam. All to make her girls—and yes, her boys at times too—feel special.

Aside from just making a memory with Amy, Molly also wanted to hear more about her friendship with Reagan, an eleven-year-old girl in the neighborhood. Amy had said some things that blipped on Molly's momma "pray-dar," and she always took those seriously, no matter how small. Amy was still sweet and innocent at nine, with no hint of the sarcasm and cynicism that seemed to be infecting younger and younger children. Molly wanted to keep her that way as long as she could.

After enjoying a first cup of tea and the treats and talking about some girl things, Molly casually inquired about Reagan while pouring a second cup. "What do you two talk about? Do you think she's a kindred spirit?" The girls especially used that literary reference when describing friends. "You said she talked about wanting to be ambitious like her mom. What do you think she meant?"

Amy added sugar and milk to her hot tea as she talked in her still-young-girl voice. "Reagan said her mom told her that if a girl really wanted to get anywhere in life, she would have to learn how to be shrewd and ambitious. What do you think about that, Mom?"

Molly took a sip of tea and prayed silently. "Well, sweetie, Jesus did say we need to be 'as shrewd as serpents,' but only in sharing the gospel with the world. He didn't mean we should be shrewd to get ahead in life or to get what we think we want." She put her teacup down. "He also said we need to be 'as innocent as doves.' He just meant we need to have pure thoughts that we don't let the world's ideas spoil. He says the world is full of wolves, and we need to be both smart sheep and good sheep."

A sly smirk came across Amy's face. "Well, I certainly don't want to be a baaaad sheep." And then with air quotes she added, "Do ewe?" Molly got it and groaned. Amy had a truly delicious sense of humor at times, a skill apparently inherited from her very punny father. They both laughed, and she added, "Don't worry, Mom. I'm happy just being an innocent sheep here at home right now."

They continued to talk for another hour or so, which gave Molly time to regale Amy with one of her famous—in the McPherson home, anyway—"Molly Tales." This one was from before she met Josh, when she was working as a staff writer in a corporate office. Her boss asked her to write a story that wasn't true. She wouldn't do it, and she was let go because of it. "Being good in God's eyes was more important to me than sacrificing my good character to get ahead."

Molly also liked to come up with her own creative illustrations. "It's like our tea and scones. God made tea and bread and jam to be 'good' to our tastes because He is good, and He gave us a good creation to enjoy. But God also made us—you and me—'good' so the world could 'taste and see that the Lord is good' by how we live. We're a picture of His goodness. If we choose not to be good—not to have good character—we'll just be like cold tea and stale scones. Does that make sense?"

Right then, Josh and Davey came back from their trip to Fogurty's. Amy stood up and said, "Thank goodness! You're just in time. I think another Molly Tale was coming." As she began to help with the tea things, she smiled at her mother. "Thanks, Mom. That was the specialest special-tea ever. The tea was hot and the scones were fresh, so it was good." For Molly, it was all good.

- *Just for Fun:* What kinds of special "eat and talk" times do your children love in your home? Tea times? Snack dinners? Hot chocolate and cookies? Pizza nights? What food gets your kids talking most?

- How do you talk about God's goodness at home? What is the relationship between God's goodness and good character? How can you cultivate God's goodness in your children?

I Interact with the Word
TRUTHS ABOUT CULTIVATING YOUR CHILD'S CHARACTER

LUKE 8:11-15 | *Good character grows in the good soil of a cultivated heart*

This is the meaning of the parable: The seed is God's word. The seeds that fell on the footpath represent those who hear the message, only to have the devil come and take it away from their hearts and prevent them from believing and being saved. The seeds on the rocky soil represent those who hear the message and receive it with joy. But since they don't have deep roots, they believe for a while, then they fall away when they face temptation. The seeds that fell among the thorns represent those who hear the message, but all too quickly the message is crowded out by the cares and riches and pleasures of this life. And so they never grow into maturity. And the seeds that fell on the good soil represent honest, good-hearted people who hear God's word, cling to it, and patiently produce a huge harvest.

Word Notes: The parable of the Sower is one of only six parables that occur in all three synoptic Gospels, and it is unique in the way it is told and interpreted by Jesus. It is an illustration of how the gospel of the Kingdom is spread and then either rejected or accepted. The "sower" is probably walking along a path through a field and sowing seed, but only the seed landing on "good soil" (that is, prepared soil) yields growth.

1. The seed of God's Word (the gospel of the Kingdom) falls on three kinds of unreceptive hearts: a hard heart (v. 12), a shallow heart (v. 13), and a divided heart (v. 14). What influences created each kind of heart soil? What are you doing as a parent to prevent those kinds of soil in your child's heart?

2. The fourth seed falls on a receptive heart (v. 15): a prepared heart with soil that has been loosened, cleared,
   and tilled. Jesus says it is, literally, a "good and good"
   heart. It is not yet a saved heart, but it is able to value
   all the goodness of God. How are you creating that
   kind of good soil in your child's heart?

3. The good heart hears the Word, clings to it, and produces much fruit. Isn't that what you want for your
   child? Jesus uses two words for "good" that suggest aes-
   thetic goodness (beauty) and ethical goodness (truth).
   How can you cultivate in your child a value for the
   goodness of beauty and truth?

2 TIMOTHY 3:14-15 | *Truth is planted in the youngest heart*

You must remain faithful to the things you have
been taught. You know they are true, for you know
you can trust those who taught you. You have been
taught the holy Scriptures from childhood, and they
have given you the wisdom to receive the salvation
that comes by trusting in Christ Jesus.

Word Notes: This passage is included as an example of good, prepared soil in a young child's life. In his final letter, Paul warns Timothy of the kinds of people who will be unfaithful to the gospel. Then Paul reminds him of all the teaching he's heard and observed and encourages him to remain faithful to what he learned from Paul and from his faithful grandmother Lois and mother, Eunice (see 1:5).

1. Timothy has followed Paul faithfully since he heard him preach the gospel in Lystra. Paul has taught and trained him for ministry, but his mother and grand-mother were also trusted as "those who taught [him]." What kind of parental relationship and teaching might cause your child to trust you that way?

2. Paul reminds Timothy that he had been "taught the holy Scriptures from childhood." He uses the term *brephos*, which refers to an infant or even a baby still in the womb. From a very early age, Timothy was taught the Scriptures. At what age do you think your child can be "taught" the Scriptures? Why?

3. The teaching Timothy received as a young child gave him "wisdom to receive the salvation that comes by trusting in Christ Jesus." The cultivation of his young heart created good soil where God's wisdom could grow and where he could receive the seed of the gospel. What kind of teaching can create wisdom that leads to salvation?

GALATIANS 5:22-25 | *The fruit of the Spirit is the character of Christ*

The Holy Spirit produces this kind of fruit in our lives: love, joy, peace, patience, kindness, goodness, faithfulness, gentleness, and self-control. There is no law against these things! Those who belong to Christ Jesus have nailed the passions and desires of their sinful nature to his cross and crucified them there. Since we are living by the Spirit, let us follow the Spirit's leading in every part of our lives.

Word Notes: The letter to the Galatian church is one of Paul's earliest epistles. He was writing primarily to confront the "Judaizers," Jewish Christians who believed certain Jewish laws were still binding on the church. Paul forcefully rejected that view and eloquently defended justification by faith, grace and freedom in Christ, and the power of the Holy Spirit to enable us to please God.

1. Paul asserts that we walk either by the flesh (by law) or by the power of the Holy Spirit. The fruit of the Spirit is Christ's character produced by the Spirit of God within us. How do your children see the "fruit of the Spirit" in your parenting? What can you do to model the fruit for them to imitate?

2. Paul says that we as believers can walk in the Spirit because the "passions and desires" of our sinful nature were crucified with Christ on the cross. Does that picture of spiritual reality ever come to your mind as a parent? How could it be used as an encouragement for you or your child to develop character?

3. Finally, Paul states very simply that if we live by the Spirit, then we should also walk by the Spirit. In other words, if God's life is in us by the Spirit, then let's let Him guide the way we live. Lifegiving parenting affirms

the same thing. How are you giving your child God's life by walking in the Spirit?

F *Focus on Parenting*
PLANS FOR CULTIVATING YOUR CHILD'S CHARACTER

FROM THE LIFEGIVING PARENT, *CHAPTER 8*

If the Sower parable includes children's hearts, as I believe it does, then Jesus' instruction for you as a lifegiving parent is clear: Your responsibility is to keep the soil of your children's hearts loosened, tilled, cleared, cultivated, and fed with the goodness of God so they will also be among those "who have heard the word in an honest and good heart, and hold it fast, and bear fruit with perseverance" (Luke 8:15, NASB). Those are words all lifegiving parents should want said of their children.

MAKE LIFEGIVING PLANS FOR YOUR FAMILY

Christian character is formed through a complex mixture of influences, values, and behaviors. It's also as simple as learning and choosing to value the goodness of God in all its expressions, being the new person that God has made you in Christ, and walking by the Spirit because you have new life

97

from the Spirit. Write out ways that the life of God in you as a lifegiving parent can influence and cultivate godly character in your child. As a group, share and compare your ideas for cultivating your children's characters.

E | *Engage with God*
PRAYERS FOR CULTIVATING YOUR CHILD'S CHARACTER

Share prayer requests related to the concepts you've discussed this week. Then move into a time of group prayer, letting these prompts direct you:

- Lord, let Your Holy Spirit work in our lives so others can see the character of Christ.

- Help us to cultivate the soil of our children's hearts with Your beautiful and true goodness.

- Even if our children are very young, let us fill their hearts with words of Your truth.

- Teach us as parents to live in the lifegiving power of the Holy Spirit for our children.

- Lord, show us how to cultivate the soil of our children's hearts with Your goodness.

FORMING YOUR CHILD'S IMAGINATION

*You will keep in perfect peace all who trust in
you, all whose thoughts are fixed on you!*

ISAIAH 26:3

From The Lifegiving Parent, *chapter 9*

*In order to become healthy and strong parts of their human
nature, [children's] imaginations must be fed and formed. And
if they are to become well-formed "Christian imaginations," they
must be tended purposely to that end. That's our responsibility
as lifegiving parents. Our children's natural, innocent curiosities
are not just seeking reasonable explanations for all their questions; they are also seeking meaning. A Christian imagination
enables our children not only to see God's truth through images,
metaphors, and symbols but also to see themselves as part of a
grand story being written by God, a story that brings ultimate
meaning to everything.*

Thoughts on Forming Your Child's Imagination

Imagination may not seem at first glance like a biblical concept. But look again. You cannot read Scripture intelligently without a mature imagination that is able to find truth and meaning in metaphors, stories, images, symbols, and all kinds of unseen and unseeable spiritual realities. Imagination is the mental faculty by which your children will believe in a God who became a man, died for a sin problem they cannot see, and now reigns in heaven as King of everything. That's why it must not be passively ignored but actively fed and formed. This week we'll consider what it means to form your children's imaginations.

Talking through L.I.F.E. Together

L *Listen to a Story*
A LIFEGIVING PARENTING MOMENT:

ABOUT ROOM FOR IMAGINATION

The sound of a ringing bell coming up the stairs at eight thirty declared to any McPhersons still sleeping that this would not be a normal Saturday—as did the familiar voice of Molly: "God is good, and it's a good morning! Get up, get dressed, get down the stairs. Breakfast is served at nine o'clock. This is the day the Lord has made. Let us rejoice and be glad in it."

Thirty minutes later, all McPhersons were dressed and

sitting around an epic morning feast—cinnamon rolls, scrambled eggs, bacon, hash browns, orange juice, and freshly ground and brewed coffee. The table was creatively decorated for fall with a basket of foliage and gourds, an autumn table runner, and pumpkin candles. Josh posted an Instagram video of the unfolding scene.

Tables like this were part of their creative life as a family. Something about a table filled with the goodness of God's creation not only fed hungry bodies but also fueled and enlivened hungry minds. Nothing could focus a discussion better than sitting around a table, facing each other and feasting together. And this was Molly's table to talk about the basement.

"As you all know, the basement below us remains partially unfinished. Which is fine, since we are all partially unfinished, so our house is just like us." This was an understanding nod to Josh, who had never gotten back to their basement once his business took off. "However, I would like to suggest that we rescue part of the basement from its increasingly disordered state. I propose that today—not sometime, but today—we begin to bring order to the family room by creating the family 'Imaginarium.'" She breathily intoned the new name with a sense of mystery and awe. There were oohs and aahs of approval from around the table.

The so-called family room at the bottom of the basement stairs, though mostly finished as a living space, had devolved over time into a mishmash of storage, project tables, play spaces, and general disorder. Molly wanted to bring order to that room by making it a creative space—a place where imagination and creativity were not just released and explored but also celebrated and enjoyed. She thought every house should have an Imaginarium.

Molly described a place where artwork could be created and displayed, music composed and performed, and literary works written and read. She paused to sip her coffee, which was a strategic error at this table of talkative family members. Amy, a budding watercolor artist, jumped into the gap. "I'd like an easel and places on the wall to hang my paintings."

Gracie, who was exploring both piano and guitar as well as songwriting, was next. "I think it would be neat to have a place to play my music, and even record it."

Davey was already writing stories and poems, illustrating them with drawings, and binding them in simple books. "Can I have a place to show my stories? That would be pretty cool."

Even T. J. jumped in. "I want a place where I can draw superheroes and put my Lego things." He was the family Lego builder of fanciful towers and complex battle scenes.

"What about you, Mom?" Gracie asked.

Molly was obviously delighted with the response to her proposal. "This is so exciting! I love all your ideas. And for me? I'd like a corner to decorate creatively every season to show God's glory and goodness, and some easels and wall space to display my photography. That would be wonderful."

"Hey, don't forget me," Josh declared. He didn't have much time for hobbies, but recently he had begun to make and edit simple but creative videos. "I'd like a place to show the world my incredibly imaginative videos. A table where I can put my laptop would do nicely."

At which Gracie said, "Oh, and you could help me make music videos. That would be so cool."

And with that, the McPherson Imaginarium was born. There was more excited talk about using leftover paint and supplies from Shedzilla to give the room a creative makeover. The rest of the day was spent bringing order to the current disorder of the room—cleaning, moving things to Shedzilla, and planning with Josh what needed to be done next. It was a family project to prepare the way for an outbreak of imagination.

- *Just for Fun:* What creative activities does each of your children most enjoy? What creative activities do your children see you enjoying? How are personal creative works displayed in your home?

- What are you doing to expand and release your children's imaginations? What are some new ways that you could display and appreciate their creative works?

I *Interact with the Word*
TRUTHS ABOUT FORMING YOUR CHILD'S IMAGINATION

GENESIS 1:26-27, 31 | *We can imagine because of the image of God*

God said, "Let us make human beings in our image, to be like us. They will reign over the fish in the sea, the birds in the sky, the livestock, all the wild animals on the earth, and the small animals that scurry along the ground." So God created human beings in his own image. In the image of God he created them; male and female he created them. . . . Then God looked over all he had made, and he saw that it was very good! And evening passed and morning came, marking the sixth day.

Word Notes: There is no question that the creation of man and woman is the pinnacle of the Genesis creation narrative. They are distinct from all other creatures because they were created by God "in his own image." Scripture doesn't define the *imago Dei* (Latin for "image of God"), but it is arguably whatever qualities make human beings different from animals—relationships, reason, will, and even imagination.

1. Although we are not told exactly what the image, or likeness, of God is, are there any clues in the first mention of it in verse 26? What aspects that are unique to humanity might be suggested by God's declaration that humans would "reign over" other creatures? How does that require imagination?

2. We are made in God's image as male and female (v. 27), created with a need for relationship. How does

our nature as relational creatures affect our imagination and creativity? When you imagine something good, what do you do? When you create something new, what do you do with it?

3. Genesis says that "God looked over all he had made" and declared it "very good." All artists will step back to examine and evaluate their creative works. What does this verse imply about God's imagination as an artistic creator? What would it mean if this were also part of His image in us?

Isaiah 26:3-4 | *God expects us to imagine what He will do*

You will keep in perfect peace all who trust in you,
all whose thoughts are fixed on you! Trust in the
Lord always, for the Lord God is the eternal Rock.

Word Notes: Only a few words for "imagination" are used in Scripture. The Hebrew term *yatsar* can mean "to form or fashion in the mind"—to frame, conceive, or imagine something unseen as real and true. In this passage, the noun form translated as "thoughts" is used. However, it is what those thoughts are about that is key. Isaiah 25:6–26:2 is all about a coming "day" when God will "swallow up death forever." This passage is about being able to imagine the reality of "that day."

1. Isaiah affirms that God will sustain the "perfect peace"—the *shalom*—of all who trust in Him. When you first hear that verse, what do the words *trust* and *peace* suggest to you? How could you change the way you act or think in order to live by these words? Where would the "perfect peace" come from?

2. In the Hebrew, the second half of the passage actually comes first. "All whose thoughts are fixed on you" is the condition for finding perfect peace. But the phrase has just two words in Hebrew: the steadfast (firm) of mind (imagination). How does that change how you hear the words? How can imagination bring peace?

3. Isaiah's second affirmation of trust in God looks back to 25:6-12, when he describes what God will do on "that

day" in the future. God is trustworthy because He is "the eternal Rock." How do you trust God for something promised that is yet to happen? How does that require your imagination?

EPHESIANS 1:16-20 | *We need the light of imagination to see God's future*

I pray for you constantly, asking God, the glorious Father of our Lord Jesus Christ, to give you spiritual wisdom and insight so that you might grow in your knowledge of God. I pray that your hearts will be flooded with light so that you can understand the confident hope he has given to those he called— his holy people who are his rich and glorious inheritance. I also pray that you will understand the incredible greatness of God's power for us who believe him. This is the same mighty power that raised Christ from the dead and seated him in the place of honor at God's right hand in the heavenly realms.

Word Notes: Paul's visionary and instructive Ephesian letter includes one of the most beautiful and inspiring prayers of the New Testament. It is filled with images, metaphors, and concepts of the blessings reserved by God for us in eternity, and it affirms the work He has done and continues to do through Christ. It is more than a prayer of propositional truth; it is an image of truth.

1. Paul prays that God will give the Ephesians "spiritual wisdom and insight" so they can grow in their knowledge of Him. He wants them to envision a personal God imparting to them not just information but also a kind of inspiration. How would you picture God in your mind based on this prayer?

2. In verse 18, Paul prays that the believers' hearts will be "flooded with light"—literally, "that the eyes of your heart may be enlightened" (NASB). What does the metaphorical "eyes of your heart" suggest about how we understand God's truth? What is the relationship between "heart eyes," light, and imagination?

3. The rest of the prayer describes aspects of the "confident hope" that Paul says we will need enlightened eyes of the heart to see. Is the hope he prays for only about

knowledge? What does he want the believers to "see" with the eyes of their hearts, or their imaginations?

F *Focus on Parenting*
PLANS FOR FORMING YOUR CHILD'S IMAGINATION

FROM THE LIFEGIVING PARENT, *CHAPTER 9*

Most Christian parents do not fear imagination, but neither do they especially respect its power in children's lives. It's easy to wrongly assign it to the category of pleasant childhood diversions that will pass in time as their children grow into young adulthood. But children's developing imaginations need to be properly fed in order to grow into mature imaginations that can anchor the deepest, most meaningful concepts in Scripture. A faith that is uninformed or uninspired by the images, metaphors, symbols, and stories of God's Word is in danger of becoming unimaginative and unanchored, weakened by an overreliance on reason, adrift on a shallow sea of facts and propositions.

MAKE LIFEGIVING PLANS FOR YOUR FAMILY

The Scripture passages we have examined have been about imagination in general, not specifically about your children's imaginations. But it is their imaginations that you as a lifegiving parent need to form so they can share, along with you, in the vision of what they can become in God's grand story. In other words, they need you to imagine so they can imagine. List some ways that you can feed and form your children's Christian imaginations. As a group, share and compare your ideas for forming your children's imaginations.

E Engage with God
PRAYERS FOR FORMING YOUR CHILD'S IMAGINATION

Share prayer requests related to the concepts you've discussed this week. Then move into a time of group prayer, letting these prompts direct you:

- Lord, expand our imaginations to strengthen our faith and hope for the coming Kingdom.

- Let Your image in us find expression and form in ways that our children can see and believe.

- Strengthen our imaginations, our *yatsars*, so that we may have *shalom* to give to our children.

❈ Lord, enlighten the eyes of our hearts so we may see all the spiritual blessings we have with You.

❈ Give us imagination, that we can be lifegiving parents and form the imaginations of our children.

ONE LIFE TO GIVE

We will not hide these truths from our children; we will tell the next generation about the glorious deeds of the LORD, about his power and his mighty wonders.

PSALM 78:4

From The Lifegiving Parent, *chapter 10*

Lifegiving is all about . . . life! It's not a program, curriculum, or set of procedures that you can follow and be done with. It's life, and life is both always being done and never done. Lifegiving parenting is organic, natural, relational, and it can even be impromptu and a bit messy. It's a mental and spiritual attitude about and toward your children. It may sound cliché to say, but lifegiving parenting is not just about what you do but is mostly about who you are. By that I mean it's not what you do that defines who you are, but who you are that defines what you do.

Thoughts on One Life to Give

Let's be clear as we wrap up this study: "One Life to Give" is not a bow to the trendy and ubiquitous #YOLO (You Only Live Once). It's about the no-longer-trendy-but-classier "Carpe diem!" As a lifegiving parent, you have a window of only about ten years before your child moves into a new stage of development and your influence changes—ten years to lay the foundation and give your child a life worth living in Christ. So "Seize the days!" This final week is about taking a step back to take stock of where you are as a parent and where you want to be. It's about taking a step forward to start making changes at home to give your child the life of the living God. It's about taking on the challenge to become a lifegiving parent.

Talking through L.I.F.E. Together

L *Listen to a Story*
A LIFEGIVING PARENTING MOMENT:

ABOUT LIGHT FOR LIFEGIVING

The opening chords of "Seize the Day" on his car radio immediately took Josh back to college. In the fall of his junior year, he heard Carolyn Arends in concert with Rich Mullins and became a lifelong fan of both Christian artists. Just listening to Arends's iconic song during the Friday Classics drive-home segment took him back to 1995. The catchy melody was now on repeat in his brain, and he couldn't get that part about life slipping away like hourglass sand out of his mind either.

The chorus was still playing in his head on Sunday as he listened to Pastor Goodson's sermon from the preamble to Psalm 78—the first eight verses instructing parents to tell their children about God so they would not forget Him. He wondered if there was a divine conspiracy to tell *him* something. He convinced himself that such a conspiracy should be confirmed only upon a trinity of supposed nudges from the Almighty. Soon he would discover that Molly was the third person in that trinity.

Sunday afternoons nearly always found the family sitting down for another McPherson tradition—the Sunday family tea time. To celebrate the fall season this week, Molly's signature dessert, to be served up with the English tea and hot chocolate, would be one of her most requested—fresh apple crisp with vanilla bean ice cream. As she was cutting apples in the kitchen, Josh came in to make conversation.

"Hey, hon. I can already taste your amazing apple crisp. Can't wait for tea time." He was working up to a question. "I noticed driving home from lunch today that you were pretty quiet. That's not like you. Is there something on your mind?"

Molly smiled and finished slicing the final apple. "Sorry, sweetie. I guess I was kind of distracted. I was just thinking about the children." Josh waited for more as she put the crisp topping on the apples. "I've been thinking about what it means to build a Christian home. We do a lot of Christian things as a family, but I think it's more than that. I wonder if we can give our children a good Christian life and yet still fail to give them the life of Christ." She put the apple crisp in the oven and turned around to face Josh. "I want to be sure our children find God's life in our home. I want us to be the kind of parents who give that life to our kids . . . lifegiving parents."

Tea time was especially lively, and Molly's apple crisp hit everyone's sweet spot. The large windows in the living room let in the afternoon sunlight, prompting Josh to mention a Bible verse. "Jesus told us that we're the light of the world. The Bible also says that God's light is His life. So if we're His light in the world, we're also His life. We give the world His life. We're lifegivers." He looked over at Molly, who was sitting next to him on the couch. "Is that what you meant in the kitchen?"

Molly nodded in agreement, but Josh still thought there was something else going on in her. "Yes, that really is what I meant. Guys, I know this might sound funny at first, but it's not enough just to *see* God's light. Jesus wants us to *be* His light. Your father and I want you to know God's life, not just know about it. That means that we, your father and I, need to give you the life we've found in God. It means we need to be what we're going to call lifegiving parents."

"And that's what we're going to be," Josh exclaimed as he put his arm around his wife. "We're going to seize the day and be lifegiving parents for you."

Molly took Josh's hand while he sang the chorus to "Seize the Day." When he finished, Molly added, "And one more thing, sweetie. Do you remember when we prayed at the lodge for God to give us more of His life that we could give to our children?" Josh nodded his head. "Well, I think He's answered that prayer." She put her hand on her stomach and gave Josh a sideward glance and a smile.

"Wait. You're not talking about what we're talking about, are you? You're talking about . . . You mean . . ." And with that, the whole room exploded in squeals of delight, and the couch filled to capacity with four excited children. Lifegiving had come, in more ways than one, to the McPherson home.

- *Just for Fun:* What songs do you associate with your college years? What would be your favorite dessert for a Sunday tea time? Mothers, how have you announced pregnancies or upcoming adoptions to your family?

- What can you start doing at home to become more of a lifegiving parent? What might be keeping you from becoming a lifegiving parent? How are you one already?

Interact with the Word
TRUTHS ABOUT ONE LIFE TO GIVE

JOSHUA 4:20-24 | *Memorial stones to remember God's faithfulness*

It was there at Gilgal that Joshua piled up the twelve stones taken from the Jordan River. Then Joshua said to the Israelites, "In the future your children will ask, 'What do these stones mean?' Then you can tell them, 'This is where the Israelites crossed the Jordan on dry ground.' For the LORD your God dried up the river right before your eyes, and he kept it dry until you were all across, just as he did at the Red Sea when he dried it up until we had all crossed over. He did this so all the nations of the earth might know that the LORD's hand is powerful, and so you might fear the LORD your God forever."

Word Notes: The Israelites are looking across the Jordan into the Promised Land. Moses has died; Joshua is the new leader. As He did for Moses with the Red Sea, God holds back the Jordan so the people can cross on dry ground. Before returning the river to its banks, God tells Joshua to take twelve stones from the dry riverbed and set them up at Gilgal as a memorial of what He has done for Israel as they enter the land.

1. The memorial stones are placed in Gilgal as a remembrance of the miracle of the Israelites crossing the Jordan on dry ground. The stones will remind them of God's faithfulness. How do you remember God's faithfulness to your family? Do you record those events in some way?

2. Though Joshua mentions the children, the memorial stones are actually for the parents. It is the parents who are to show the stones to their children and explain what they mean. What are the memorial stones in your home, literally or figuratively? When do you visit the "stones" with your children to explain them?

3. Joshua says the stones are also a testimony of God's powerful hand to "all the nations of the earth" and a testimony to the Israelites that He is worthy of their fear. How can God's faithfulness to your family become a testimony to others? How can your children share their own parts in that testimony?

PSALM 78:4-7 | *Telling the children God's truth so they tell their children*

We will not hide these truths from our children; we will tell the next generation about the glorious deeds of the LORD, about his power and his mighty wonders. For he issued his laws to Jacob; he gave

his instructions to Israel. He commanded our
ancestors to teach them to their children, so the next
generation might know them—even the children
not yet born—and they in turn will teach their own
children. So each generation should set its hope
anew on God, not forgetting his glorious miracles
and obeying his commands.

Word Notes: Asaph, author of twelve psalms, was a leading
musician of Israel during the reign of King David, about three
centuries after Joshua's time. In Psalm 78, Asaph recounts the
wayward history of Israel, concluding with David as God's
trusted shepherd. In his preamble (vv. 1-8), he hearkens back
to the words of Moses and Joshua, reaffirming that the future
of Israel is in the hands of its parents.

1. Asaph echoes the words of Joshua in verse 4—telling
    the next generation about God's power and works.
    Now that there is at last stability in the land, Asaph
    reminds Israel's parents to tell their children the truths
    of God. How can we inadvertently hide truth from our
    children? How can we be sure to "tell" them?

2. In verses 5-6, Asaph recalls Moses' giving Israel the Shema (Deuteronomy 6:4-9), with its instructions for parents to teach their children God's truths so they will do the same for future generations. How do you think about faith generationally? What can you do now to begin a generational chain of faith?

3. Asaph reminds the people of Israel that the generational chain of faith must start fresh with each new generation of families (v. 7). How are you renewing your hope in God in your children? How do you remember His faithfulness and talk about being faithful? What can you do to make that a priority?

JOSHUA 24:14-15 | *As for me and my family, we will serve the LORD*

Fear the LORD and serve him wholeheartedly. Put away forever the idols your ancestors worshiped when they lived beyond the Euphrates River and in Egypt. Serve the LORD alone. But if you refuse to serve the LORD, then choose today whom

you will serve. Would you prefer the gods your
ancestors served beyond the Euphrates? Or will it
be the gods of the Amorites in whose land you now
live? But as for me and my family, we will serve the
LORD.

Word Notes: Joshua took over the leadership of Israel after
Moses' death and led the people into the land promised to
Abraham five hundred years earlier. Now the fighting is over
and there is rest in the land. Joshua, old and ready to retire,
has called the people together at Shechem so he can deliver a
final farewell address, where he will charge them to be faithful to the Lord and serve Him only.

1. After recounting all that God has done for Israel,
    Joshua charges the people to "fear the LORD and serve
    him wholeheartedly." God has done even more for us
    in Jesus, so what does it mean for us as Christians to
    fear God and serve Him? What does it mean to do that
    "wholeheartedly"?

2. Then Joshua challenges the people to reject the gods
    and idols their ancestors worshiped and choose to
    "serve the LORD alone." What spiritual idols can Chris-
    tians hold on to (for example, Paul calls greed idolatry)?

How can modern idolatry affect our lifegiving parenting and our children?

3. Although Joshua makes clear that the people will have to make their own choices, he says, "As for me and my family, we will serve the LORD." How can you, as a Christian family, publicly declare your choice to serve Jesus? How can your children hear your testimony as a lifegiving parent to serve the living God?

 ### *F* *Focus on Parenting*
PLANS FOR ONE LIFE TO GIVE

FROM THE LIFEGIVING PARENT, *CHAPTER 10*

If you want to be a faithful and lifegiving parent, know that your God is faithful. Here's a verse to keep in mind: "Without faith it is impossible to please Him, for he who comes to God must believe that He is and that He is a rewarder of those who seek Him" (Hebrews 11:6, NASB). Let me break that down to some simpler terms for this priority: Have faith, faithfully trust God, trust in God's faithfulness. The priority to know your God as faithful is an anchor—it will keep you from drifting away from being the lifegiving parent you want to be.

MAKE LIFEGIVING PLANS FOR YOUR FAMILY

You have only one life to give for your children, one time to "seize the day" for them. Once the window of childhood closes, you won't have a second opportunity to be the kind of lifegiving parent they will have only one chance to have. But remember that lifegiving parenting flows both ways—your children will receive more life from God, and you will too! Lifegiving parenting is good for children and for parents. Whatever you give now, you will receive back in blessings and joy—first from your children who follow God because of the life they receive through you at home, and second from God for being a lifegiving parent who follows Him. It's a win-win choice.

So to echo Joshua, choose today how you will serve your lifegiving Lord as a lifegiving parent. To keep it simple, think about all we've studied and discussed and write down three ways (just three) that you can begin giving your children the life of the living God. Start your journey of lifegiving parenting today. As a group, share and compare your ideas for becoming a lifegiving parent.

E | *Engage with God*
PRAYERS FOR ONE LIFE TO GIVE

Share prayer requests related to the concepts you've discussed this week. Then move into a time of group prayer, letting these prompts direct you:

✳ Lord, give us vision to "seize the days" of our children's lives in order to give them Your life.

✳ Help us to create memorial stones in our families that will remind us of Your faithfulness.

✳ Let us never forget that through our own lives, we are giving Your life to future generations.

✳ Lord, may we choose today to serve You—not the gods of our culture but You alone.

✳ We commit our hearts to You today; we're ready for the journey of lifegiving parenting.

Meeting as a Lifegiving Parents Group

Planning

- Identify couples you think might be interested in a group like this. If you need ideas, check with your church leadership.
- Host an evening to describe the study and discuss how the group might be structured.
- Create an e-mail list or Facebook group for interested couples.
- Agree together on a regular meeting time and create a calendar to send to all the members.
- Decide if you will meet at one home or rotate between homes.
- Purchase or order this study guide in advance of the first meeting. Group members may also want their own copies of *The Lifegiving Parent*.
- If you're the group organizer, send a reminder e-mail for each meeting.
- Decide as a group whether or not you will arrange for any childcare and how payments, if any, will be handled.

Leading

- Always begin the formal study at the agreed-upon starting time.
- Be careful to stay close to the suggested time for each segment so you can end the meeting on time.
- It is not necessary to answer every question in the Bible discussion section. However, even if you don't get to every question, be sure to read each Scripture passage.
- For the prayer segment, remind group members to keep prayers related to the topic of the study for that meeting.
- As the leader, close the prayer segment to be sure you end on time.

Meeting

- If you are hosting a meeting, plan ahead for beverages and snacks.
- If some parents have babysitters at home and don't want to be out too late, it's better to fellowship before the study instead of afterward.
- Have the meeting area for the group arranged and set up ahead of time.
- If the group members don't all know each other, provide name badges.
- For those who stay later, feel free to set a "time to say good night" time.

Knowing the Lifegiving God

If you want to be a lifegiving parent but you're not sure if you know the lifegiving God, the Bible has good news for you. It starts with a verse you've probably heard many times before:

> This is how God loved the world: He gave his one
> and only Son, so that everyone who believes in him
> will not perish but have eternal life.
>
> JOHN 3:16, JESUS SPEAKING

But why would someone perish? Because of sin. "For everyone has sinned; we all fall short of God's glorious standard" (Romans 3:23). Sin separates everyone from God, and without forgiveness of sin, we will die and not spend eternity with God. That's the bad news. But here's the good news: God, because He loves us, has provided a solution for sin in His Son, Jesus. He offers eternal life. Here's what various writers in the New Testament say about Jesus' words:

- *This is how God loved the world . . .*
  "God showed his great love for us by sending
  Christ to die for us while we were still sinners."
  (Romans 5:8, Paul)

- *He gave his one and only Son . . .*
  "Christ suffered for our sins once for all time. He
  never sinned, but he died for sinners to bring you

safely home to God. He suffered physical death, but he was raised to life in the Spirit." (1 Peter 3:18, Peter)

- *so that everyone who believes in him . . .*
"Whoever has the Son has life; whoever does not have God's Son does not have life. I have written this to you who believe in the name of the Son of God, so that you may know you have eternal life." (1 John 5:12-13, John)

- *will not perish . . .*
"God is so rich in mercy, and he loved us so much, that even though we were dead because of our sins, he gave us life when he raised Christ from the dead. (It is only by God's grace that you have been saved!)" (Ephesians 2:4-5, Paul)

- *but have eternal life.*
"[Jesus said,] 'I tell you the truth, those who listen to my message and believe in God who sent me have eternal life. They will never be condemned for their sins, but they have already passed from death into life.'" (John 5:24)

Did you hear the solution? If you're not sure if you know the lifegiving God, you just need to believe in Jesus to have God's life now and when you die. "Whoever has the Son has life." Believe in Jesus. That's all. God will take it from there. If you want the full story, read the Gospel of John.

About the Authors

Clay Clarkson is the executive director of Whole Heart Ministries, the nonprofit Christian home and parenting ministry he and Sally founded in 1994. He has been the administrator for more than sixty ministry conferences since 1996 and is the publisher at Whole Heart Press, the publishing arm of the ministry. He has written, cowritten, and edited numerous books, and he considers himself an expository writer with a heart for communicating truth and wisdom from God's Word to strengthen Christian parents and families. Clay earned a master of divinity from Denver Seminary in 1985 and ministered on church staffs overseas and in the States before starting Whole Heart Ministries. He is also a Christian singer, songwriter, and worship leader, and he is currently developing children's illustrated storybook concepts. He and Sally have lived in fifteen homes in two countries and four states in their thirty-seven years of marriage. They now live at 7,300' in Monument, Colorado, in the shadow of Pikes Peak.

Sally Clarkson is the mother of four wholehearted grown children, a champion of biblical motherhood, and a visionary inspirer of Christian women. Her ministry reaches thousands of women every day on the SallyClarkson.com blog and AtHomeWithSally.com podcast, and by her presence on social media. She is the author or coauthor of twenty books, a popular conference speaker for more than twenty years, the heart of Mom Heart Ministry small-group outreach to mothers and Mum Heart Ministry international, and the voice of the LifeWithSally.com monthly online-streaming media subscription course for Christian women. Her recent books *The Lifegiving Home* (with Sarah Clarkson) and *The Lifegiving Table* capture her belief in and commitment to the power of home in the life of children. Sally thrives on the companionship of her family, thoughtful books, beautiful music, regular tea times, candlelit dinners at home, good British drama, walking, and traveling to see her children.

Clarkson Family Books and Resources

The Lifegiving Home: Creating a Place of Belonging and Becoming
Sally Clarkson and Sarah Clarkson (Tyndale, 2016)

The Lifegiving Home Experience: A 12-Month Guided Journey
Sally Clarkson with Joel Clarkson (Tyndale, 2016)

The Lifegiving Table: Nurturing Faith through Feasting, One Meal at a Time
Sally Clarkson (Tyndale, 2017)

The Lifegiving Table Experience: A Guided Journey of Feasting through Scripture
Sally Clarkson with Joel Clarkson and Joy Clarkson (Tyndale, 2017)

Different: The Story of an Outside-the-Box Kid and the Mom Who Loved Him
Sally Clarkson and Nathan Clarkson (Tyndale, 2017)

A Different Kind of Hero: A Guided Journey through the Bible's Misfits
Sally Clarkson and Joel Clarkson (Tyndale, 2017)

Own Your Life: Living with Deep Intention, Bold Faith, and Generous Love
Sally Clarkson (Tyndale, 2014)

Heartfelt Discipline: Following God's Path of Life to the Heart of Your Child
Clay Clarkson (Whole Heart Press, 2003, 2012, 2014—3rd ed.)

Our 24 Family Ways: A Family Devotional Guide
Clay Clarkson (Whole Heart Press, 1998, 2004, 2010, 2014)

Our 24 Family Ways: Kids Color-In Book
Clay Clarkson (Whole Heart Press, 2004, 2014)

Educating the WholeHearted Child: WholeHearted Christian Home Education for Ages 4–14
Clay Clarkson with Sally Clarkson (Apologia Press, 1996, 1998, 2011—3rd ed.)

10 Gifts of Heart: What Your Child Needs to Take to Heart before Leaving Home
Sally Clarkson (Whole Heart Press, 2013, 2017)

The Mission of Motherhood: Touching Your Child's Heart for Eternity
Sally Clarkson (WaterBrook Press, 2003)

The Ministry of Motherhood: Following Christ's Example in Reaching the Hearts of Our Children
Sally Clarkson (WaterBrook Press, 2004)

Create a home where your children will experience the living God in your family.

In *The Lifegiving Parent*, respected authors and parents Clay and Sally Clarkson will equip you with the tools and wisdom you need to give your children much more than just a good Christian life. You'll give them the life of Christ.

www.tyndale.com

Available wherever books are sold and online

CP1364

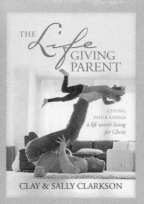

WHOLE HEART MINISTRIES™

Whole Heart Ministries is a nonprofit Christian home and parenting ministry founded by Clay and Sally Clarkson. Since 1994, our mission has been to encourage, equip, and enable Christian parents to raise wholehearted children for Christ. As a family-run ministry, our goal has been to help Christian parents through books and resources, events, and online ministries. Our current ministry initiatives include Sally Clarkson Ministry, Mom Heart Ministry, Storyformed Project, Family Faith Project, and the WholeHearted Learning Project.

For more information, visit our ministry websites or contact us.

WholeHeart.org—Information, vision, and heart of Whole Heart Ministries

SallyClarkson.com—Sally's blog, podcast, and more for Christian women

LifeWithSally.com—Monthly courses from Sally's two decades of ministry

MomHeart.com—Training and encouragement for Mom Heart small groups

Storyformed.com—Blog and resources on reading and literature for families

MyFamilyFaith.com—Blog, helps, and resources on family faith formation

Whole Heart Ministries
PO Box 3445
Monument, CO 80132

719-488-4466 | 888-488-4466
whm@wholeheart.org | admin@wholeheart.org

CP1362